TOWARDS A TRUE SPIRITUAL CONNECTION

A Translation of *iḍāʾātun fī maʿnā al-irtibāṭ*

Wisdom from the Teachings of
Habib ʿUmar bin Hafiz

MUHAMMAD BIN ʿABDULLAH BIN ʿALI AL-AYDARUS

Translated by **Abdullah Salih**

TITLE: TOWARDS A TRUE SPIRITUAL CONNECTION

ISBN: 978-1-952306-67-9

FIRST EDITION | AUGUST 2024

AUTHOR: MUHAMMAD BIN ʿABDULLAH BIN ʿALI AL-AYDARUS

PROOFREADING: KELLY ELYAQOUBI

COVER DESIGN: ISKANDAR DZ

TYPESETTING: IGP CONSULTING | WWW.IGPCONSULTING.COM

DISTRIBUTION: WWW.SATTAURPUBLISHING.COM | INFO@SATTAURPUBLISHING.COM

WWW.IMAMGHAZALI.CO

[**INTERIOR:** PHOTO OF ḤABĪB ʿUMAR BİN ḤAFĪẒ COURTESY OF ADAM SBITA WITH THE REQUEST OF DUAS FOR HIM & HIS FAMILY]

CONTENTS

A Brief Biography

Ḥabīb ʿUmar bin Ḥafīẓ

HIS STUDY OF THE ISLAMIC SCIENCES

Ḥabīb ʿUmar was born in Tarīm, in Yemen's Ḥaḍramawt Valley. He is a direct descendant of the Messenger of Allah ﷺ through Imām al-Ḥusayn. His father and his father's father and all his forefathers were scholars and knowers of Allah. Among his blessed forefathers are Imām ʿAlī Zayn al-ʿĀbidīn as well as the first of the Prophetic Household to settle in Ḥaḍramawt, Imām Aḥmad bin ʿĪsā al-Muhājir and his noble descendants, al-Faqīh al-Muqaddam Muḥammad bin ʿAlī, Sheikh ʿAbd al-Raḥmān al-Saqqāf and Sheikh Abū Bakr bin Sālim. His full lineage is as follows:

He is al-Ḥabīb al-ʿAllāmah ʿUmar bin Muḥammad bin Sālim bin Ḥafīẓ bin ʿAbdullāh bin Abū Bakr bin Aydarūs bin ʿUmar bin Aydarūs bin ʿUmar bin Abū Bakr bin Aydarūs bin al-Ḥusayn bin al-Sheikh al-Fakhr Abū Bakr bin Sālim bin ʿAbdullāh bin ʿAbd al-Raḥmān bin ʿAbdullāh bin Sheikh ʿAbd al-Raḥmān al-Saqqāf bin Sheikh Muḥammad Mawlā al-Dawīlah, bin ʿAlī Mawlā al-Darak, bin ʿAlawī al-Ghayūr, bin al-Faqīh al-Muqaddam Muḥammad, bin ʿAlī, bin Muḥammad Ṣāḥib Mirbāṭ, bin ʿAlī Khālī Qasam, bin ʿAlawī, bin Muḥammad Ṣāḥib al-Ṣawmāʿah, bin ʿAlawī, bin ʿUbaydullāh, bin al-Imām al-Muhājir il-Allāh Aḥmad, bin ʿĪsā, bin Muḥammad al-Naqīb, bin ʿAlī al-ʿUrayḍī, bin Jaʿfar al-Ṣādiq, bin Muḥammad al-Bāqir, bin ʿAlī Zayn al-ʿĀbidīn, bin Ḥusayn al-Sibt, bin ʿAlī bin Abī Ṭālib and Fāṭimah al-Zahrāʾ, the daughter of our Master Muḥammad, the Seal of the Prophets ﷺ.

HIS STUDY OF THE ISLAMIC SCIENCES

At an early age, Ḥabīb ʿUmar memorized the Qurʾān and began studying the Islamic sciences under his father and many of the great scholars of Tarīm of the time. Among them were Ḥabīb Muḥammad bin ʿAlawī bin Shihāb, Ḥabīb Aḥmad bin ʿAlī Ibn Sheikh Abū Bakr, Ḥabīb ʿAbdullāh bin

Sheikh al-Aydarūs, Ḥabīb ʿAbdullāh bin Ḥasan Balfāqīh, Ḥabīb ʿUmar bin ʿAlawī al-Kāf, Ḥabīb Aḥmad bin Ḥasan al-Ḥaddād, Ḥabīb Ḥasan bin ʿAbdullāh al-Shāṭirī and his brother, Ḥabīb Sālim, the Muftī, Sheikh Faḍl bin ʿAbd al-Raḥmān Bā Faḍl, and Sheikh Tawfīq Amān. He also studied under his older brother, Ḥabīb ʿAlī al-Mashhūr, who was the Muftī of Tarīm.

HIS MIGRATION TO AL-BAYḌĀʾ

In 1387 (1967), a socialist government came to power in South Yemen which attempted to eradicate Islam from society. Scholars were persecuted and religious institutions were forcibly closed. In spite of this, Ḥabīb ʿUmar's father, Ḥabīb Muḥammad, fearlessly continued calling people to Allah. He was required to register with the security forces on a regular basis so that they could check on his whereabouts. Thus, on Friday morning on 29th Dhu'l-Ḥijjah 1392 (1973) he left Ḥabīb ʿUmar, then only nine years of age, in the mosque before the Friday prayer and went to register. He was never seen again. Ḥabīb ʿUmar remained in Tarīm under the care of his blessed mother, Ḥabābah Zahra bint Ḥafīẓ al-Ḥaddār and his older brother, Ḥabīb ʿAlī al-Mashhūr. The situation in Ḥaḍramawt became increasingly difficult and thus in Ṣafar 1402 (1981), Ḥabīb ʿUmar migrated to the city of al-Bayḍāʾ in North Yemen, safe from the socialist regime in South Yemen.

He resided in the Ribāṭ of al-Bayḍāʾ and studied at the hands of the founder of the Ribāṭ, the great Imām, Ḥabīb Muḥammad bin ʿAbdullāh al-Ḥaddār, as well as Ḥabīb Zayn bin Ibrāhīm bin Sumayṭ, the Ribāṭ's main teacher. Ḥabīb Muḥammad held him in high regard and could see the future that was awaiting him. He duly married his daughter to him. Ḥabīb ʿUmar inherited his father's passion for teaching people and calling them to Allah ﷻ, and he had begun this noble work at the age of fifteen, but it was in al-Bayḍāʾ that he had the opportunity to work freely. He had a great impact on the youth of the city and was a means for many of them to become students in the Ribāṭ, then scholars, and callers to Allah ﷻ. He established a number of weekly lessons and gatherings of knowledge. He would often travel in order to call to Allah ﷻ in the area around al-Bayḍā', just as he would travel further afield to al-Ḥudaydah and Ta'izz. He used to frequently visit Ta'izz in order to take knowledge from the great scholar, Ḥabīb Ibrāhīm bin 'Aqīl bin Yaḥyā.

HIS REPEATED VISITS TO THE ḤIJĀZ

During his time in al-Bayḍā', Ḥabīb 'Umar made frequent visits to the Ḥijāz. There he learnt from the great Imāms of the time: Ḥabīb 'Abd al-Qādir al-Saqqāf, Ḥabīb Aḥmad Mashhūr al-Ḥaddād, and Ḥabīb Abū Bakr al-'Aṭṭās al-Ḥabašī. He took license to narrate from the chains of transmission in Hadith and in other sciences from Sheikh Muḥammad Yāsīn al-Faddānī and the Hadith scholar of the Two Sanctuaries, Sayyid Muḥammad bin 'Alawī al-Mālikī, as well as other scholars.

HIS MOVE TO OMAN AND AL-SHIḤR

After the fall of the socialist regime in 1410 (1990) and the unification of North and South Yemen, Ḥabīb 'Umar returned to Ḥaḍramawt. He visited Tarīm, and then settled with some of his students in the city of Ṣalālah in the Sultanate of Oman. For a year and a half, he called people to Allah in the region and then in 1413 (1992) he moved to the city of al-Shiḥr, which lies on the Indian Ocean in the province of Ḥaḍramawt.

The Ribāṭ of al-Mustafā had recently been reopened after closure during the days of the socialist regime. Ḥabīb 'Umar began teaching in the Ribāṭ and reviving its traditions. Many students from different regions of Yemen and parts of South-East Asia came to seek knowledge from him.

HIS RETURN TO TARĪM

Ḥabīb 'Umar then returned to his home city and immediately began to breathe new life into the religious life of the region. His tireless work led to the establishment of Dār al-Mustafā in 1414 (1994).

Dār al-Mustafā is a center for traditional Islamic learning based upon three foundations: the first is *'ilm* (knowledge), learning the sciences of the Sacred Law from those who are qualified to impart them through connected chains of transmission; the second is tazkiyah, purifying the soul and refining one's character; and the third is da'wah, calling to Allah and conveying beneficial knowledge.

Dār al-Mustafā began in Ḥabīb 'Umar's house next to the Mawlā 'Aydīd mosque, and a batch of students from South East Asia came to study with him, as well as students from Tarīm and other parts of Yemen. As the number of students increased, the need for a purpose-built building became clear. Land was duly purchased and building started. Dār al-Mustafā was officially opened in 1417 (1997).

Ḥabīb 'Umar honored his father's sacrifice by making the opening date 29th Dhu'l-Ḥijjah, the day on which Ḥabīb Muḥammad was abducted. Although Dār al-Mustafā was established recently, it is intimately connected to the illustrious legacy of the scholarly tradition of Ḥaḍramawt, which stretches back more than a thousand years. In this, we witness the renewal of the religion (tajdīd) that is taking place at the hands of Ḥabīb 'Umar.

Dār al-Zahrā' was opened in 1422 (2001) to provide learning opportunities for women as well. A number of branches of Dār al-Mustafā have since been opened in Ḥaḍramawt and South East Asia. A branch has been opened in the Yemeni capital, Ṣan'ā', and older ribāṭs have also been revived, such as the ribāṭs of al-Shiḥr, Mukallā', and 'Aynāt.

Dār al-Mustafā and its branches continue to grow and receive students from all corners of the earth.

HIS TRAVELS

Ḥabīb 'Umar constantly travels to convey the Prophetic message and to call people to Allah. He delivers regular lectures and khuṭbahs within Ḥaḍramawt and often makes trips abroad. His travels have taken him to almost all the Arab states, East and South Africa, South East Asia and Australia, the Indian Subcontinent, Western Europe and Scandinavia, and North America. He has connected to the chains of transmission of the scholars of these regions and has also participated in many Islamic conferences.

HIS WRITINGS AND PUBLICATIONS

Although Ḥabīb 'Umar is best known for his speeches and lessons, he has authored several works. Among them are *al-Dhākirah al-Musharrafah*, which contains personally obligatory knowledge for every Muslim, and three short Hadith compilations, *Mukhtār al-Ḥadīth, Nūr al-Īmān, and Quṭūf al-Fāliḥīn*. His *Qabas al-Nūr al-Mubīn* is a summarized version of the third quarter of Imām al-Ghazālī's *Iḥyā' 'Ulūm al-Dīn* and is an expression of his concern for curing the ailments of the heart. It also reflects the love and respect that the Bā 'Alawī scholars have traditionally had for *Iḥyā' 'Ulūm al-Dīn*. A selection of Ḥabīb 'Umar's speeches and wisdoms have been collected in *Tawjīhāt al-Ṭullāb* and *Tawjīh al-Nabīh*, and some of his khuṭbahs have been collected in *Fayḍ al-Imdād*. *Khulāṣat al-Madad al-Nabawī* is Ḥabīb 'Umar's compilation of adhkār for the seeker to recite on a daily basis. It contains Prophetic invocations and the litanies of many of the great Imāms. His mawlid compositions, *al-Ḍiyā' al-Lāmi'* and *al-Sharāb al-Ṭahūr* are recited in gatherings throughout the world, as are his poems.

TOWARDS A TRUE

SPIRITUAL CONNECTION

A Translation of *iḍāʾātun fī maʿnā al-irtibāṭ*

Wisdom from the Teachings of

Habib ʻUmar bin Hafiz

إِضَاءَاتٌ فِي مَعْنَى الِارْتِبَاطِ

العلامة الحبيب عمر بن حفيظ

In the Name of Allah the Beneficent, the Merciful

All praise is due to Allah ﷻ who said, "...and for every nation there is a guide", and may salutations and peace be upon the best guide of all, the one who nurtured the servants and helped them to achieve the pinnacle of culture and guidance – our Master Muhammad ﷺ – who said, "My Lord taught me manners and He taught me manners well". May the peace of Allah ﷻ be upon his family who received the radiant light of guidance, who are protected and pure of all filth and deviation, and may Allah ﷻ be pleased with all his companions, who followed the path of prophethood and who were people of great virtue and chivalry.

Since the right upon the seekers of those who nurture the seekers is enormous and only those whose hearts are pure and who are steadfast upon the path of perfection will be able to recognise and fulfil it, I would like to mention some pearls of wisdom from the teachings of our nurturer and teacher, Habib 'Umar bin Hafiz, in this short treatise. I hope it would enable us to recognise the right of being in the company of those whose condition inspires us and whose words guide us towards Allah ﷻ so that we too could hold on to divine attributes, be imbued with prophetic characteristics, and imbibe the qualities of the true servants.

Those who have the title Nuturer (*Murabbī*) are the ones who show the seekers how to reach Allah ﷻ because they are the heirs and inheritors of the very first reformer and *Murabbī*, regarding whom Allah ﷻ said, "Just like we sent among you a Messenger who recites before you Our verses, reforms you and teaches you the Book and the Wisdom, and who teaches you that which you did not know".

مُقَدِّمة

بِسْمِ ٱللَّهِ ٱلرَّحْمَٰنِ ٱلرَّحِيمِ

الحمد لله القائل ﴿وَلِكُلِّ قَوْمٍ هَادٍ ۝٧﴾ [الرعد: ٧]، والصلاة والسلام على خير هاد، مربّي العباد، وموصلهم إلى غاية الأدب والرشاد، سيدنا محمد القائل «أدبني ربي فأحسن تأديبي»، وسلام الله تعالى على أهل بيته المتلقين أنوار الهداية، المحفوظين المطهرين عن الرجس والغواية، ورضي الله تعالى عن أصحابه السائرين على منهج النبوة، أولي المكارم والفتوة.

أما بعد، لما كان حقُّ المربين على المريدين كبير، ولا يعرفه ويؤديه إلا من تصفى له الضمير وثبت قدمه في المسير.. أحببنا نقل بعض من كلام مربِّينا وشيخنا سيدي الحبيب عمر بن محمد بن سالم بن حفيظ بن الشيخ الفخر أبي بكر بن سالم في هذه الورقات المعدودة، حتى نعرف حق صحبة الرجال الذي ينهضنا حالهم، ويدلنا على الله مقالهم، فنكون بأوصاف الربوبية.. متعلقين، وبشمائل النبي.. متخلقين، وبصفات عبوديتنا.. متحققين.

فالمربُّون: هم دليل الله إليه؛ لكونهم ورثة المربِّي المزكِّي الأول ﷺ، الذي قال عنه ربه: ﴿كَمَآ أَرْسَلْنَا فِيكُمْ رَسُولًا مِّنكُمْ يَتْلُواْ عَلَيْكُمْ ءَايَٰتِنَا وَيُزَكِّيكُمْ وَيُعَلِّمُكُمُ ٱلْكِتَٰبَ وَٱلْحِكْمَةَ وَيُعَلِّمُكُم مَّا لَمْ تَكُونُواْ تَعْلَمُونَ ۝١٥١﴾ [البقرة: ١٥١].

The ones who took up the responsibility of this effort after the Messenger of Allah ﷺ are his heirs, and they did this in order to ensure that this distinctive feature of the *ummah*, the blessed group of Nurturers, remains. Their very existence is a means of safety and when they are no more... the Qur'an will be taken from this earth. Our leader, Imam al-Haddād ﵀ said, "Had they not been among the people, the mountains would have shattered because of the amount of sin being committed".

Whoever hands himself over to them will be freed from the shackles of his own carnal self and from the plots and scams of the Devil and his armies, and he will return to the special natural disposition upon which Allah ﷻ had created him. Thereafter, he will ascend to the stages and levels of conviction and proximity to the Lord of the Worlds.

We therefore beseech Allah ﷻ to enable us to benefit from the spiritual conditions and speech of our sheikh and teacher so that we are also granted manners and etiquette, so that we are protected from perdition and so that we can ascend to the highest stages with complete ease.

Servant of the Da'wah Academy at Darul Mustafa,
Muhammad bin 'Abdullah bin 'Ali al-Aydarus

وقام بحق هذا الأمر بعد رسول الله ﷺ.. ورثته؛ ليبقى لهذه الأمة خصوصيتها في وجود هذه الثُّلة المباركة من المربين، فوجودهم أمان، وعند فقدهم.. سيُرفع القرآن، قال سيدنا الإمام الحداد:

ولولاهم بين الأنام لدكدكت جبال وأرض لارتكاب الخطيئة

ومن سلم لهم زمامه.. خرج عن طبع نفسه، وعن كَيْد الشيطان وجنوده، وعاد إلى خصوصية فطرته التي فطره الله عليها، ثم يترقَّى بعد ذلك إلى مقامات اليقين والقرب من رب العالمين.

فنسأل الله أن ينفعنا بحال وكلام شيوخنا حتى نُرزق الأدب ونُحفظ من العَطَب ونرقى أعلى الرتب في عافية.

خادم الدائرة الدعوية بدار المصطفى

محمد بن عبد الله بن علي العيدروس

The definition of "sheikh"

My teacher ﷺ said, "A sheikh is someone whose internal connects with your internal; your heart is filled with immense honour for his instructions and your feet are steadfast in following his path".

My teacher ﷺ also said, "He is the one who helps you to reach the King of Kings from within the bounds of physical matter and what we see, and this is achieved through repentance".

The condition of the murīds with the sheikhs[1]

Whilst reading from the book 'Awārif al-Ma'ārif, my teacher ﷺ said, "In this chapter, the author is discussing the etiquettes of the murīds when they are in the company of their sheikhs. The door to their connection and the key to their divine assistance are their sheikhs. all the way up their chain until the very jewel of all creation, the one ﷺ who connects us to the Most Loving Lord, and the one ﷺ who will enter into the Court of Allah Most High along with the delegations of the righteous by means of etiquette, honesty, and true testimony – May the peace and salutations of Allah ﷻ be upon him.

However, the very end of this chain and the door to this assistance is the sheikh you directly derive benefit from. This is why the most important etiquettes are those that apply to the murīds when they are in the company of their sheikhs. This is because they are tantamount to good manners and etiquette with Allah ﷻ and with His Messenger ﷺ, with divine revelation, with the Pure Sacred Law and with the Divine Path or spiritual reformation. This is why they consider it so important.

The pious people would determine the success of a *murīd* by the quality of his etiquettes and they were of the view that if he has perfected his etiquette he will definitely inherit the divine gift of proximity to Allah ﷻ and understanding of what Allah ﷻ has gifted that sheikh, proportionate to his etiquette.

---

1 *Murīd refers to the one who comes to the* sheikh desiring spiritual reformation.

تعريف الشيخ :

قال سيدي رَضِيَ اللَّهُ عَنْهُ: والشيخ: هو الذي اتّصل سرُّك بسرِّه، وامتلاء قلبُك بتعظيم أمره، وثبت قدمك على اتباع سيره.

وقال سيدي أيضاً: الشيخ: هو الذي يوصلك إلى ملك الملوك من حصر المادة والمظاهر فتتحقق بالتوبة.

حال المريدين مع الشيوخ:

ومما قال سيدي رَضِيَ اللَّهُ عَنْهُ أثناء القراءة في كتاب عوارف المعارف:

يتحدث في هذا الباب عن أدب المريدين مع الشيوخ، فإنه باب سندهم، ومفتاح مددهم، شيوخهم إلى زين الوجود، وهو -صَلَّى اللَّهُ عَلَيْهِ وَسَلَّمَ- الموصل إلى الرب الودود، والداخل بالوافدين إلى حماه على وجه الأدب والصدق وحسن الشهود على إلههم المعبود، صلوات الله وسلامه عليه.

ولكن طرف هذا السند وباب هذا المدد.. الشيخ الذي تتلقى عنه، فلهذا كان من أهم الآداب.. أدب المريدين مع الشيوخ؛ لأنه يُترجِم الأدب مع الله والأدب مع رسوله صلَّى الله عليه وصحبه وسلَّم، والأدب مع الوحي المنزل، والأدب مع الشريعة الغراء، والأدب مع المنهاج الإلهي، فلأجل هذا كان من المهام عندهم.

وكانوا يستدلون على نجاح المريد.. بحسن أدبه، ويرون أنه إذا كَمُل منه الأدب.. فلابد أن يرث من سرِّ الاقتراب من الحق والفهم عنه مما حبا الله ذلك الشيخ الحظ والنصيب الأوفر بحسب أدبه.

Abu 'Abdullah al-Suhrawardi رحمه الله said, "The best education regarding this etiquette is what Allah ﷻ taught the very first people in this *ummah* to derive benefit from the Prophet ﷺ. Allah said, "O you who believe! Do not proceed before Allah and His Messenger..." Allah ﷻ did not say: Do not proceed before the Messenger of Allah. Rather, He said, "Do not proceed before Allah and His Messenger". They did not proceed in any matter before Allah. How could they proceed with anything in any case!? However, proceeding in any matter before receiving an instruction from the Messenger ﷺ has been regarded as poor etiquette and bad manners with Allah ﷻ. Therefore, bad etiquette before the Messenger of Allah ﷺ is tantamount to bad etiquette before Allah Himself!

The reason Allah ﷻ said, "Do not proceed before Allah and His messenger..." is that some of the companions wanted to be safe with regards to fasting in Ramadhan (not to miss a fast) and, therefore, they started fasting before the Messenger of Allah ﷺ and before Ramadan. Some of them also slaughtered their sheep before him ﷺ on the day of Eid and, when a religious matter was presented, some of them started offering a view regarding it before he ﷺ spoke. There was also an incident in which some of the companions started having a heated debate in his presence and started raising their voices.

This is when Allah ﷻ revealed verses to teach them good manners and etiquette. Allah ﷻ said, *"O you who believe! Do not proceed before Allah and His messenger and fear Allah. Indeed, Allah is the All-Hearing, the All-Seeing. O you who believe! Do not raise your voices above the voice of the Prophet, nor speak loudly to him as you do to one another lest your deeds are made void while you are unaware. Indeed, those who lower their voices in the presence of the Messenger of Allah are the ones whose hearts Allah has refined for righteousness. They will be granted forgiveness and a great reward. Indeed, those who call out to you (O Prophet) from outside your private quarters, most of them have no understanding (of basic etiquette). Had they been patient until you come out to them, it would have certainly been better for them and Allah is the Oft-Forgiving, the Most Merciful"(al-Hujurat, 1-5).*

Thus, this verse encompasses all the etiquettes that the Companions of Allah's most beloved ﷺ were required to imbibe and which spread among those treading the path towards the proximity of Allah ﷻ throughout

وقال -أي أبو عبد الله السهروردي-: أن الأصل في هذا الأدب.. ما أدب الله المتلقين الأوائل من الأمة عن سيد المرسلين صلَّى الله عليه وصحبه وسلَّم، خير من تُلُقّيَ عنه ﴿يَـٰٓأَيُّهَا ٱلَّذِينَ ءَامَنُوا۟ لَا تُقَدِّمُوا۟ بَيْنَ يَدَيِ ٱللَّهِ وَرَسُولِهِۦ﴾ لم يقل: لا تقدموا بين رسول الله، ولكن قال ﴿لَا تُقَدِّمُوا۟ بَيْنَ يَدَيِ ٱللَّهِ وَرَسُولِهِۦ﴾، وهم ما يُقدِّمون بين يدي الله شيء، كيف يتقدمون في شيء؟! ولكن جُعِل التقدم على رسول الله.. إساءة أدب مع الله سُبْحَانَهُ وَتَعَالَىٰ، **فإساءة الأدب مع النبي.. إساءة أدب مع الرب.**

فقال: ﴿لَا تُقَدِّمُوا۟ بَيْنَ يَدَيِ ٱللَّهِ وَرَسُولِهِۦ﴾ وذلك لأن بعضهم أراد الاحتياط فتقدم في الصوم قبله قبل رمضان، وبعضهم ضحَّى قبله في يوم العيد، وبعضهم إذا عُرضت المسألة.. خاض فيها قبل أن يتحدث صلَّى الله عليه وصحبه وسلَّم، وبعضهم تلاحوا في مجلسه حتى ارتفعت أصواتهم، فنزل الأدب من الرب ﴿يَـٰٓأَيُّهَا ٱلَّذِينَ ءَامَنُوا۟ لَا تُقَدِّمُوا۟ بَيْنَ يَدَيِ ٱللَّهِ وَرَسُولِهِۦ ۖ وَٱتَّقُوا۟ ٱللَّهَ ۚ إِنَّ ٱللَّهَ سَمِيعٌ عَلِيمٌ ۝١﴾، ﴿يَـٰٓأَيُّهَا ٱلَّذِينَ ءَامَنُوا۟ لَا تَرْفَعُوٓا۟ أَصْوَٰتَكُمْ فَوْقَ صَوْتِ ٱلنَّبِيِّ وَلَا تَجْهَرُوا۟ لَهُۥ بِٱلْقَوْلِ كَجَهْرِ بَعْضِكُمْ لِبَعْضٍ أَن تَحْبَطَ أَعْمَـٰلُكُمْ وَأَنتُمْ لَا تَشْعُرُونَ ۝٢ إِنَّ ٱلَّذِينَ يَغُضُّونَ أَصْوَٰتَهُمْ عِندَ رَسُولِ ٱللَّهِ أُو۟لَـٰٓئِكَ ٱلَّذِينَ ٱمْتَحَنَ ٱللَّهُ قُلُوبَهُمْ لِلتَّقْوَىٰ ۚ لَهُم مَّغْفِرَةٌ وَأَجْرٌ عَظِيمٌ ۝٣ إِنَّ ٱلَّذِينَ يُنَادُونَكَ مِن وَرَآءِ ٱلْحُجُرَٰتِ أَكْثَرُهُمْ لَا يَعْقِلُونَ ۝٤ وَلَوْ أَنَّهُمْ صَبَرُوا۟ حَتَّىٰ تَخْرُجَ إِلَيْهِمْ لَكَانَ خَيْرًا لَّهُمْ ۚ وَٱللَّهُ غَفُورٌ رَّحِيمٌ ۝٥﴾ [الحجرات: ١-٥].

فكانت مجامع الآداب.. تحلَّى بها الأحباب مع سيد الأحباب، وانتشرت في أهل الاقتراب زمناً بعد زمن ووقتاً بعد وقت، وبعد نزول الآيات حصلت الأثر في الصحابة، فمنهم سيدنا أبو بكر وسيدنا عمر صار لا يكاد يُسمع لهما صوت في حضرة رسول الله، حتى أن أحدهما ليسأله أحياناً فلا يدري ما قال من شدة مخافتته

the ages. After this verse was revealed, it had an immediate and indelible effect on the companions. Luminaries like Abu Bakr رضي الله عنه and Umar رضي الله عنه were so affected by this verse that, from the moment they heard it, they lowered their voices when in the blessed company of the Prophet ﷺ to the extent that one could barely hear them speak. In fact, at times they would ask a question and the Prophet ﷺ would have to ask "What did you say?" because of how softly they spoke. This was their condition.

Another example is that of Thābit رضي الله عنه who actually had a naturally booming voice. However, when this verse was revealed, he was overcome with tremendous fear and he said, "I am almost certain that all my deeds have been nullified, because Allah ﷻ said, "Do not raise your voices above the voice of the Prophet, nor speak loudly to him as you do to one another lest your deeds are made void"". He was so worried that he could not bring himself to leave his home and secluded himself for a number of days out of fear.

Look at the effect that this verse had on them and what their response was to Divine Revelation. He was unable to leave his home until the Prophet ﷺ noticed that he was not present for one, two, and then three days. Then, he ﷺ asked: "Who will find out what happened to Thābit?" One of the companions stood up and volunteered to go.

He thus went to the home of Thābit رضي الله عنه and called out, "O family of Thābit! Where is Thābit?" His family responded saying, "He is right here in his room. For the last three days he has been praying at home and we have been following him in prayer. He does not speak to anyone. All he does is cry. You may enter and meet with him".

He entered the house and said, "Peace be upon you". He replied saying: "May peace be upon you too". The visitor then said, "The Messenger of Allah ﷺ has sent me to you". "Has something been revealed about me?!" he asked out of fear, "Has Allah ﷻ revealed verses reprimanding me?!" "No, No!" said the visitor, "He was wondering where you were because he hadn't seen you. Why have you not come to him?" He replied, "By Allah! It is only because of this verse, and you know very well that I have a booming loud voice. I am convinced that all my deeds have been wiped out and I am an inmate of the Hellfire. I can't eat, or drink, or even sleep and for the last three days I have not even left my home either".

بالصوت، فيقول : «ما قلت؟»، فهكذا كان حالهم.

ومنهم سيدنا ثابت، وسيدنا ثابت كان جهوري الصوت، أي صوته في حد ذاته مرتفع، فلما نزلت الآية.. نازله الخوف الشديد، وقال: ما أظنني إلا قد حبط عملي ﴿وَلَا تَجْهَرُواْ لَهُۥ بِٱلْقَوْلِ كَجَهْرِ بَعْضِكُمْ لِبَعْضٍ أَن تَحْبَطَ أَعْمَٰلُكُمْ﴾ فنازله من ذلك هَمٌّ شديد فلم يقدر على الخروج من البيت، واعتكف خائفاً.

انظر إلى تأثير الآيات عليهم، وكيفية أحوالهم مع الوحي كيف يكون!

فما عاد قدر يخرج من البيت حتى افتقده النبي صلَّى الله عليه وصحبه وسلَّم في اليوم الأول والثاني والثالث، فقال: «من يأتيني بخبر ثابت»، فذهب بعض الصحابة قال: أنا يا رسول الله.

فذهب إلى بيته فنادى: يا آل ثابت، أين ثابت؟ فكلمه أهله قالوا له: هذا هو ثابت أمامك في الغرفة له ثلاثة أيام يقوم إلى الصلاة نصلي معه ولا يكلمنا وهو يبكي محله فادخل عليه.

فدخل عليه فقال: السلام عليكم، فردّ: وعليكم السلام، قال: أرسلني إليك رسول الله، قال: أَنَزَل فيَّ شيء؟ هل نزل فيَّ شيء من الله تعالى عتاباً؟

قال: لا لا، افتقدك فهو يسأل عنك.

ما أخَّرك عنه؟ قال: والله ما هو إلا هذه الآية، وأنت قد عرفتني جهير الصوت وما أظنني إلا أنه قد حبط عملي وأنني من أهل النار، ولهذا ما استطعت لا آكل ولا أشرب ولا أنام ولا أخرج من البيت اليوم الأول والثاني والثالث.

رأيت الأثر كيف يكون!! فرجع إلى النبي، وقال له: يقول ثابت كذا كذا، فقال:

Can you see what an effect it had on him?!

The visitor went back to the Prophet ﷺ and told him exactly what Thābit رضي الله عنه had said.

The Messenger of Allah ﷺ replied: "Go back and tell Thābit that he is a dweller of Paradise!"

He, therefore, went to Thābit رضي الله عنه and conveyed the glad tidings to him saying, "The Messenger of Allah ﷺ said that you are a dweller of Paradise. You are not going to Hell". He was elated, suddenly regaining his ability to stand, and immediately set out to meet the Prophet ﷺ.

Allah ﷻ says, *"O you who believe! Do not proceed before Allah and His Messenger and fear Allah. Indeed, Allah is the All-Hearing, the All-Seeing"* (*al-Hujurat*, 1) – He ﷻ is basically telling us, I hear you and I know what is in your hearts when you are before the Prophet ﷺ. One of you raises his voice and the other proceeds prematurely in certain matters or actions... I hear and see you, so do not treat My beloved like this! Do not behave like this with My Prophet ﷺ.

Thus, they were not allowed to do anything before the Prophet ﷺ - not fasting, not slaughtering an animal, and not even walking in front of the Prophet ﷺ unless there was clear permission from Allah ﷺ as is well known with regards to his battles and other aspects of his life.

How to build this connection

My teacher – may Allah be please with him – said, "Building this connection depends on two things:

1. True and honest love
2. Humility

Whoever you find to be like this should be looked after very well. Whoever you find like this, direct him to action and do not fear for him because he will be strong and steadfast as long as he remains connected. The purer his is, the more he will drink from the proverbial cup. The best thing you can do is to enter the fold of those who are in this field. Serving them to the best of your ability is the most powerful tool you can possess".

My teacher also said, "As for a connection with the Pious People, it depends on four things:

«ارجع إليه وقل له: إنه من أهل الجنة»، فجاء إليه وبالبشارة وقال: قال لك رسول الله ﷺ: «إنك من أهل الجنة» إنك لست من أهل النار، فسُرِّي عنه وتماثل للقدرة على القيام فخرج إلى رسول الله صلَّى الله عليه وعلى آله وصحبه وسلَّم.

﴿يَٰٓأَيُّهَا ٱلَّذِينَ ءَامَنُواْ لَا تُقَدِّمُواْ بَيْنَ يَدَيِ ٱللَّهِ وَرَسُولِهِۦۖ وَٱتَّقُواْ ٱللَّهَۚ إِنَّ ٱللَّهَ سَمِيعٌ عَلِيمٌ ۝١﴾ [الحجرات: ١]، قال: أنا أسمعكم وأعلم ما في قلوبكم بين يدي النبي، واحد منكم يرفع الصوت وواحد منكم يتقدم عليه في أمر أو في عمل، أنا سميع عليم أمامكم لا تفعلوا هكذا مع حبيبي، لا تفعلوا هكذا مع نبي صلَّى الله عليه وعلى آله وصحبه وسلَّم، إلى آخر ما ذكر.

فما كان لهم أن يتقدموا في صيام ولا في أضحية ولا أن يمشوا أمامه إلا حين يأتي الأمر لهم بالمضي والمشي بعد ذلك كما معروف في غزواته وبعض أحواله عليه الصلاة والسلام. اهـ.

حصول الرابطة:

قال سيدي رضي الله عنه: الرابطة ترجع إلى:

١- صدق المحبة.

٢- والتواضع.

فمن وجدته كذلك.. فالرعاية له عظيمة، من وجدته كذلك.. حطّه في العمل ولا تخاف عليه، ما دام مربوط.. كان مضبوط، وكل ما كان أصفى.. كان الكأس له أوفى.

الانطواء في أهل هذا الميدان.. أحوى لكم، والخدمة بكل المستطاع.. أقوى لكم.

1. Connecting the hearts
2. Following and obeying
3. Resemblance
4. Fulfilling their instructions

Remember, the one who these sheikhs represent ﷺ is the greatest of all creation and he said, "Whoever obeys the leader has obeyed me and whoever obeys me has obeyed Allah". Therefore, obedience to our sheikhs amounts to obedience to the Messenger of Allah ﷺ and obedience to him ﷺ amounts to obedience to Allah ﷻ".

How gatherings are supposed to be

My teacher – may Allah be pleased with him – said that gatherings are according to what the most senior person in them determines. Therefore, all gatherings are not the same and all participants are not the same. Gatherings depend on those who attend.

The Path to Allah is inherited, heart to heart

My teacher – may Allah be pleased with him – said, "The scholars of old used to say: **Whoever does not endear himself to the people of Divine Recognition will never draw near to Allah**". It is through the scolding of our beloved teacher Zain that Allah granted us a connection. Thus, whoever says: I want to reach Allah but I do not want to connect myself to the heirs (of this connection), is like someone who says: I would like to enter Paradise but I do not want to pass by *Riḍwān* (the Gate Keeper of Paradise).

If we look at who we are affiliated to and we understand the meaning of our interaction with him, it becomes compulsory for us to absolve ourselves of any trajectories or associations that are for or to anyone besides Allah ﷻ and, because of this, we should take the Prophets, the righteous and the angels as our friends. If we are true in this, we will attain the ultimate success of this world and the Hereafter.

وقال سيدي أيضاً: أما الارتباط بالمشايخ:

١- فبتعلق القلوب.

٢- مع الإقتداء.

٣- والتشبه.

٤- وإنفاذ الأمر، والمنوب عنه صلَّى الله عليه وصحبه وسلَّم أعظم الخلائق هو الذي يقول لنا: «من يطع الأمير.. فقد أطاعني، ومن أطاعني.. فقد أطاع الله» فشيوخنا طاعتهم.. من طاعته، وطاعته.. من طاعة الله تعالى.

كيفية المجالس:

قال سيدي رَضِيَ اللهُ عَنْهُ: المجالس تكون على حسب ما خصّها بها الأعلى، فلا المجالس سواء، ولا المُجالسين سواء، المَجالس.. من حيث الجليس.

الطريق إلى الحق عن طريق الورثة:

قال سيدي رَضِيَ اللهُ عَنْهُ: وقديماً قالوا: (**من لا تقرّب لأهل المعرفة.. ما قرب**)، بختنا بالحبيب وقع زين، الله يرزقنا صحة الانتساب، فالذي يقول: أريد أن أصل إلى الحق ولا دخل لي بالورثة، كمن يقول: أريد دخول الجنة ولا دخل لي برضوان.

إذا نظرنا إلى انتمائنا.. نعرف معنى تعاملنا معه، يجب أن نترفَّع عن جميع الاتجاهات والولاءات لغير الرب، ومن أجله نوالي أنبياءه وأولياءه وملائكته، وإذا صدقنا في ذلك.. ففيه سعادة الدنيا والآخرة.

The need for spiritual connection

My teacher – may Allah be please with him – said that "every single person is in need of a spiritual connection or relationship and realizing this is a great favour and blessing from Allah... and he who seeks shall find." The objective is not good deeds themselves, nor supernatural manifestations or outward appearances, nor is it to make people talk. Rather, you will achieve divine proximity through sheer divine grace and bounty and when the meaning of being connected to Allah fills every part of your mind, the desire to reach Allah dominates your being, and you lose all forms of pride and arrogance. This is because Allah says, '*Indeed, Allah does not love the arrogant and boastful*' (*Luqmān*, 18), and when you remove from yourself the roots of deception and illusion and light permeates and emanates from your heart... that is when you will draw nearer to the proverbial full moon and you will be ready to meet Him on the Day of Resurrection. You will finally reach the gathering place that the pious predecessors have spoken about in the poem: 'And make a gathering for us in the Gardens of Paradise'.

This is what Imam al-Haddād ﵁ refers to in the poem:

O my Lord! Gather us and our loved ones in Firdaus
The most wonderful Abode You have made for us.

The gatherings of great Imams like Imam al-Haddād ﵁ are truly special gatherings and the position they hold in the sight of Allah, the Great, the Exalted, is truly most honourable. How many people who are far from Allah are brought nearer by means of these gatherings, how many heedless people are brought back to reality, how many people who are asleep are woken up, how many of those who are flying on this Path are blessed with reaching their destination, and how many participants are blessed with a connection with Allah by means of various different spiritual manifestations which we are both unable to even explain or understand! Therefore, these great sheikhs look for those who have the beautiful attributes mentioned above—those who have a strong bond— because they want to crown them. They look out for us and worry about us more than what we look out for and worry about them.

الحاجة للارتباط:

قال سيدي رضي الله عنه: أمر الارتباط.. يحتاج إليه الجميع، والإدراك لهذا المعنى.. من منّة الوسيع وبركة الشفيع، ومن جدَّ.. وجد.

ما المقصود ذات الأعمال ولا مظاهر ولا أشكال ولا قيل ولا قال، لكن تدركون قربكم من ذي الإفضال وجزيل النوال، وينتشر في مناحي فكركم معنى الاتصال، ويغلب على مطلبكم ذوق الوصال، وينفك عنكم الزهو والاختيال ﴿إِنَّ ٱللَّهَ لَا يُحِبُّ كُلَّ مُخْتَالٍ فَخُورٍ ۝١٨﴾ [لقمان: ١٨]، وتنزع عنكم مقالع وجذور الغرور، ويسطع في القلوب النور، فتدنوا من حضرة بدر البدور، وتتهيأوا للجمعية في يوم النشور، وتنتهي بمجمع يطلب مثل قولهم: (واجعل لنا في الجنان مجمع)، وهو ما أشار إليه الإمام الحداد بقوله:

يا رب واجمعنا وأحباباً لنا   في دارك الفردوس أطيب موضع

فإن أمثال هذا الإمام الحداد.. مجامعهم مميّزه، ومراتبهم بتخصيص الكبير الأعلى.. معزّزه، فكم من بعيد.. يُقرَّب، وكم من غافل.. يذكّر، وكم من نائم.. يوقظ، وكم من واقف.. يُجرى به، وكم من جاري.. يطار به، وكم من طائر.. يحلّ برج الوصول، وكم من حال.. ينازله البر الوصول بأنواع من التجلّي يضيق عنها المقول ونطاق العقول.

فهم يبحثون عن أهل الأوصاف الزينة، الذين لهم تعلّق قوي؛ لأنهم يريدوا أن يتوّجونهم، بَحْثُهم عنّا وانتباههم منّا.. أكثر من بَحْثِنا وانتباهنا.

Handing over the reins to them

My teacher – may Allah be please with him – also said, "Only he who hands the reins over to someone who has already succeeded will succeed. He who hands his reins to someone who has not succeeded... how will he ever succeed?"

How to win the favour of your sheikh

My teacher – may Allah be pleased with him – said, "A *murīd* can win the favour of his sheikh by doing the following:

1. Annihilating himself by strict obedience to the sheikh's instructions.
2. Doing the tasks assigned to him.
3. Filling his heart with love.
4. Filling his heart with brotherhood and mutual respect for the sake and pleasure of Allah.
5. Setting aside his own objective, purpose, and planned trajectory for the objective, purpose, and trajectory of his sheikh.

Rule: In the middle of your heart, write "Be with Allah"... that is enough.

How to achieve sincerity with Allah

My teacher – may Allah be pleased with him – said, "Sincerity with Allah will never be achieved unless the *murīd* is humbled by falling into one of the following three categories:

1. He is a person of knowledge.
2. He is a person who loves the pious.
3. He is a person in a position and who has a following".

Deriving assistance from the pious

My teacher – may Allah be please with him – said, "Establishing a connection and relationship with the pious is already a means of deriving assistance from them, either by means of

1. Them physically assisting you.

تسليم الزمام:

قال سيدي رَضِيَ اللَّهُ عَنْهُ: **إنما ينجح ويفلح.. من سَلَّم زمامه لمفلح، ومن لم يسلِّم لمفلح.. كيف يفلح.**

حصول النظر من الشيخ:

قال سيدي رَضِيَ اللَّهُ عَنْهُ: ويحصل المريد على النظر من شيخه:

١- بتفانيه بالقيام بالأمر.

٢- وتنفيذ المهمة.

٣- وامتلاء قلبه بالمحبة.

٤- والأخوة والإجلال في الله.

٥- وأفنى مقصوده ومراده ووجهته.. في مقصود ومراد ووجهة شيخه.

قاعدة: [اكتب وسط قلبك (**كونوا معه**).. بس يكفيك].

تحقق الصدق مع الله:

قال سيدي رَضِيَ اللَّهُ عَنْهُ: لا يتحقق الصدق مع الله.. إلاّ بالخفض للمريد بحرف أو بإضافة أو بتبعية، فأما المخفوض بالحرف.. فصاحب العلم، وأما المخفوض بالإضافة.. فالمحب، وأما المخفوض بالتبعية.. فصاحب الإقتداء.

نصرة أهل السرّ:

2. Them giving you words of wisdom which benefit you.
3. Them giving preference to you over themselves.
4. You following in their footsteps".

How to follow the sheikh

My teacher – may Allah be pleased with him – said, "Following the sheikh requires:

1. True loyalty and allegiance to Allah.
2. Sincere obedience.

The more you are true in following the sheikh, the stronger your connection to him will be even though you are physically very far away, because real proximity is the proximity of the souls".

Connecting your actions with the chain of Prophethood

My teacher – may Allah be pleased with him – said, "The more connected deeds are to the chain of prophethood, the more blessed they will be. To us, a little is not a little at all so do not be frightened when you see others doing a lot when it comes to outward displays of worship or material possessions. You just focus on your relationship – pay careful attention to it and make every effort necessary to foster it. If you do that, you will be successful in this world and the next, literally and figuratively".

The correct etiquette with sheikhs

My teacher – may Allah be pleased with him – said, "We need to learn the correct etiquette when interacting with sheikhs. Our sheikhs and your sheikhs are the people of goodness. Some of them are apparent, people of high status in the sight of Allah, but the greatest of all of them, the original and the source of the sheikhs, is the best of all creation, the Prophet Muhammad ﷺ. None of the Companions reached Allah until the Prophet ﷺ was more beloved to them than their own selves and even cold water. The same applies to the followers of the Companions and the way they

قال سيدي رضي الله عنه: فالارتباط بأهل السر نصرتهم:

١- بالنفس.

٢- والنفيس.

٣- وإيثارهم.

٤- والاقتداء بهم.

كيفية اتِّباع الشيخ:

قال سيدي رضي الله عنه: يكون اتِّباع الشيخ:

١- بصدق الولاء لله.

٢- وصدق الاتباع.

وكلما كنت أصدق اتباع.. كنت أقوى ارتباط وإن كنت بعيد المسافة، القرب قرب الأرواح.

ربط الأعمال بسلسلة النبوة:

قال سيدي رضي الله عنه: **الأعمال مهما كانت مربوطة بسلسلة النبوّة.. كانت مبروكة**، والقليل عندنا.. لا يقال له قليل، فلا تهولك الكثرة ولا المظهر ولا المادة. ابحث كيف تكون صلتك.. فتحسن النظر في ذلك وتبذل غاية الوسع، فإذا عملت بذلك.. فأنت الناجح الفالح دنيا وأخرى حسّاً ومعنى.

annihilated themselves in the love of the Companions. In fact, this even applies to the relationship that existed between the Companions themselves! For example, Ibn ‘Abbās رضي الله عنه would not even knock on the door of his sheikh, Zaid bin Thābit رضي الله عنه but would rather wait outside until he was covered in dust. This is the lineage of our spiritual connection by means of the rope of love. You will never find a connection to the spiritual light of the Prophet of Allah ﷺ if you do not connect yourself to the rope of the sheikh". My teacher also said, "The best etiquette that a *murīd* can display with his sheikh is to remain silent, quiet, and still until the sheikh starts. There will be goodness and rectitude for him in his words and deeds if he does this.

Remain silent until you
have been asked a question, then say:
I have no knowledge and so
Hide behind the guise of ignorance".

He also discussed the meanings behind the words of Allah: "*Do not precede before Allah and His Messenger...*" (*al-Hujurat*, 1) and said, "Never ever seek or aspire within yourselves to reach a position better or higher, or think that you have concluded an opinion regarding any matter whatsoever that is better or more correct than the Messenger of Allah ﷺ, or the seniors of his followers such as his Companions or the pious elders. This is why Allah said, "*Do not precede before Allah and His Messenger*".

Another subtle meaning in this verse is that the murīd should always be wary of their carnal selves whispering to them about a status or rank above the sheikh or even higher. That is a sign that they will fall off the path and that Allah ﷻ does not want them. This is because Allah ﷻ only accepts the downtrodden and broken-hearted. He ﷻ only accepts those who are well-mannered and display the proper etiquette before His verses, His signs and the creation at large, even the animals and inanimate parts of nature... in general, but more so with His most special person – Muhammad ﷺ. How do you think we should then behave with those who are our link to him ﷺ? How do you think we should treat the rope of love that leads to him ﷺ? Thus, the one who does not give the sheikh his due

الأدب مع الشيوخ:

قال سيدي رَضِيَ اللَّهُ عَنْهُ:

نتعلَّم الأدب مع شيوخنا، وشيوخنا وشيوخكم أهل الخير، منهم أهل الظاهر وأهل مراتب عُلا وأبو الجميع وأصلهم ومصدرهم سيّد الوجود.

وما أحد وصل من الصحابة إلا لمّا كان النبي أحب إليه من نفسه ومن الماء البارد، وكذلك التابعين من تفانيهم في محبة الصحابة، بل حتى بين الصحابة بعضهم البعض، فابن عباس لا يضرب باب شيخه زيد بن ثابت إلى أن يسّفه التراب.

هذه سلاسل الارتباط بالاتصال الباطني بحبل المحبة.

لا يوجد ارتباط بنور الرسول.. إلاّ بالارتباط بحبل الشيخ.

وقال سيدي أيضاً: فأحسن آداب المريد مع الشيخ.. السكوت والخمود والجمود حتى يبادئه؛ لما له فيه من الصلاح قولاً وفعلاً.

ولازم الصمت إلا إن سُئلت فقل لا علم عندي وكن بالجهل مستتر

وتكلَّم عن معاني في قول الله ﴿لَا تُقَدِّمُواْ بَيْنَ يَدَيِ ٱللَّهِ وَرَسُولِهِۦ﴾ لا تطلبوا منزلة أو تحدثكم أنفسكم بمنزلة فوق أو أعلى، أو تظنوا أنكم بشأن من الشؤون أهدى إلى ما هو أصوب من رسول الله صلَّى الله عليه وآله وصحبه وسلَّم ومن الأكابر من أصحابه وخيارهم، فقال: ﴿لَا تُقَدِّمُواْ بَيْنَ يَدَيِ ٱللَّهِ وَرَسُولِهِۦ﴾.

وإن من دقائق المعنى في هذا.. أن يحمي المريدون نفوسهم من أن تحدثهم برتب فوق الشيخ ومنازل فوقه؛ فإن ذلك علامة الفشل وعلامة أن الله لا يريدهم، فإن الله جل جلاله إنما يقبل المنكسرة قلوبهم، وإنما يقبل المتأدبين مع آياته ومع شعائره ومع عموم

right in terms of etiquette will never attain proximity to Allah ﷻ. This is a ploy of the Devil which he uses to prevent people from attaining the true realities of faith (*imān*) and proximity to Allah ﷻ ... a ploy that many people fall prey to in that he convinces them to think that they are more guided and more knowledgeable than their sheikh.

This is why you will find that whoever remains aloof will be deprived of the blessings of the pious predecessors as well that of the sheikhs and seniors of his time proportionate to the extent that he thinks he is more guided, more knowledgeable, has more foresight, and has deeper understanding or that he has come to realizations that the sheikhs have not. This is the reason he will be deprived and this is why he will remain in the cage of delusion regarding his own intelligence and knowledge, until he loses complete sight of himself or Allah ﷻ wakes him up to his deviation and he repents from his false belief and the misconception that had dominated him. This is when he will humble himself and submit and receive all the goodness and blessings he had been missing out on in the past".

My teacher also said, "The pious people used to say: 'Whoever does not spend time in the company of those who have attained proximity to Allah will never attain proximity themselves; and whoever does not spend time in the company of those who have reached Allah will never reach Him either'. They also said, 'If you don't spend time in the gatherings of those who are successful, how will you succeed? If you never see the face of a successful person, how will you become successful?' However, the sheikhs mourned even more and were even more pained by the condition of a person who had every opportunity to sit in the company of the righteous and pious people of his time and area, but who was deprived of engaging with them with the proper etiquette. They would say: 'This is the ultimate deprivation'.

Think about this, though: If it is a calamity and misfortune to be deprived of the inspiration to sit in the company of the pious, then spending time with them and attending their gatherings while displaying poor or even bad manners and etiquette is an even greater deprivation and an even worse calamity. May Allah protect us! Do you not see in the words of Allah: *"Had they been patient until you come out to them, it would have certainly been better for them..."* (*al-Hujurat*, 5) It would have been a means of divine

خلقه حتى الحيوانات والجمادات عامة ومع خاصتهم خاصة فكيف مع السند إليه، فكيف مع الحبل الموصل إليه.

فمن لم يعطه حقَّه من الأدب.. لم يُحَصِّل القربة من الرب ﷻ وتعالى في علاه.

وهذا من مكائد الشيطان لكثير من الناس يصدهم عن إدراك حقائق الإيمان والقرب من الرحمن بخواطر نفوسهم أنهم أهدى أو أعلم.

ولهذا تجد كل ممن يَخلُف من الناس.. يُحرَم من بركات من سلف ومضى ومن حضر في زمانه من الأكابر بقدر ما يظن أنه أهدى أو أنه أعرف أو أنه أبعد نظراً أو أنه أدق فهماً أو أنه تنبَّه لما لم يتنبهوا له؛ فبذلك يُحرَم وبذلك لا يَزال في قيد غروره بعقله ومعلوماته حتى تنطمس بصيرته أو يتداركه الرحمن فيتنبه لِغَيِّه، ويرجع عن معتقده الباطل ووهمه الذي كان يغلب عليه، فيخضع ويذل، فيتدارك بعد أن فاته خيرٌ كثير ومددٌ كبير في ماضي أعماره.

وقال سيدي أيضاً:

قالوا: إن من لم يصحب أرباب القرب.. لا يقرب، ومن لم يصحب الواصلين.. لم يصل.

وقالوا: **من لم يجالس مفلحاً . فكيف يفلح، ومن لم يرى وجه مفلح.. فكيف يفلح.**

ورَثَوا بعد ذلك أكثر وتألموا أكبر على حال من تيسَّر له المجالسة للأصفياء والأولياء في زمانه ومكانه ثم حُرِم الأدب معهم، وقالوا: هذا حرمان أكبر، فإن كان حرمان مجالسة الصالحين.. مصيبة، فإن الجلوس معهم مع فقد الأدب معهم ومع إساءة الأدب بحضرتهم.. حرمان أكبر ومصيبة أعظم والعياذ بالله تعالى.

favour being bestowed upon them, for mercy to be shown to them, for their status to be elevated, for their hearts to be reformed, and for their internal selves to be purified, or the distance between them and Allah ﷻ to be folded up and for calamities to be removed from them – *It would have been better for them!*

However, they squandered all of it because they were impatient and because they raised their voices when they called "O Muhammad, come out!" This is what Allah ﷻ taught him. Allah ﷻ says: *"Indeed, those who call out to you (O Prophet) from outside your private quarters, most of them have no understanding (of basic etiquette). Had they been patient until you come out to them, it would have certainly been better for them and Allah is the Oft-Forgiving, the Most Merciful"* (*al-Hujurat*, 4-5). This is with reference to the delegation from the Banu Tamīm tribe when they came to Madinah and said, "Praising us is an adornment for the one who praised us and rebuking us is a disgrace to the rebuker". Thus, in this verse, Allah ﷻ has basically told them: This is Allah. When He ﷻ praises someone, that person would be lucky and fortunate to have received divine favour and would be elevated to the highest levels and loftiest positions. However, if Allah rebukes or shames someone, that person would be disgraced, rejected, humiliated and condemned to the lowest of the low. This verse tells them that this is Allah ﷻ, the Elevator, the Humiliator, the Giver, the Withholder, the Promoter, the Abaser, the One Who Harms, the One Who Benefits – Magnificent indeed is His magnificence!

Furthermore, since they were very grandiose about their spokesman and poet, Hassan bin Thābit ؓ was called for and their spokesman's poetry faded into oblivion in the face of Hassan's poetry. The youth of the *Muhājirūn* and *Anṣār* came to speak and their prose faded into nothingness in the face of the oratory skills of these Muslim youth. This is the fate of those who are pompous and self-righteous about what they have. No matter how well they achieved in the past, they have to face some kind of downfall so that they may be humbled. Said otherwise, some of those who were destined for eternal damnation were unmatched and seemingly invincible in the start until their ill-fortune was finalised at which point they were overpowered in this world and the next. May Allah ﷻ protect us from such a fate – *Āmīn*!

ألا ترى إلى قول الله: ﴿وَلَوْ أَنَّهُمْ صَبَرُواْ حَتَّىٰ تَخْرُجَ إِلَيْهِمْ لَكَانَ خَيْرًا لَّهُمْ﴾، لكان سببًا لإفاضة الجود عليهم، ووصول الرحمة إليهم، واعتلاء درجاتهم، وصلاح ضمائرهم، وتصفية سرائرهم، وطيِّ المسافة عنهم، وإبعاد الآفة منهم ﴿لَكَانَ خَيْرًا لَّهُمْ﴾،

لكن ضيعوا هذا كله بعدم صبرهم ورفعهم أصواتهم وندائهم عليك:

يا محمد اخرج إلينا، هذا مما علمه الله ﴿إِنَّ ٱلَّذِينَ يُنَادُونَكَ مِن وَرَآءِ ٱلْحُجُرَٰتِ أَكْثَرُهُمْ لَا يَعْقِلُونَ ۝٤ وَلَوْ أَنَّهُمْ صَبَرُواْ حَتَّىٰ تَخْرُجَ إِلَيْهِمْ لَكَانَ خَيْرًا لَّهُمْ ۚ وَٱللَّهُ غَفُورٌ رَّحِيمٌ ۝٥﴾ [الحجرات: ٤-٥] .

وكان هذا الحال من وفد بني تميم لما جاؤوا وقالوا: إن مدحنا زين وذمنا شين، قال لهم: هذا الله، فإذا مدح أحد.. سعد وهني بواسع الإفضال وارتقى إلى المراتب العوال، وإذا ذم أحد.. خسئ وطُرد ودُحر ونزل إلى أسفل السافلين، قال هذا هو الله تبارك وتعالى الخافض الرافع المعطي المانع المقدم المؤخر الضار النافع جل جلاله؛ وهكذا.

ولما كانوا مغرورين بخطيبهم وشاعرهم جاء سيدنا حسان بن ثابت، فما وقع شعرهم شيء أمامه، وجاؤوا شبان المهاجرين والأنصار خطبوا فما كانت خطابتهم شيء أمامهم، وهكذا تكون نهايات المغترين بما عندهم، مهما كان لهم سابقة خير.. فإنه لا بد أن يَذلَّ الأمر عندهم حتى يرجعون إلى الذل، وإلا بعض من سبقت عليه الشقاوة.. فقد لا يظهر من يغلبه في البداية حتى تَحِقَّ شقاوته ثم يُغلب دنيا وآخرة، والعياذ بالله سبحانه وتعالى.

يقول الشيخ -أي أبو عبد الله السهروردي:

في هذا تأديب للمريد في الدخول على الشيخ والإقدام عليه، مشيراً إلى أن جميع

Sheikh Abu 'Abdillāh al-Suhrawardi رضي الله عنه said that this verse contains a lesson for the murīd regarding how he should visit his sheikh and proceed in his presence. This is also an indication to the fact that all the manners and etiquettes that the people of *Taṣawwuf* have implemented and taught are derived from the Noble Qur'an and the Inimitable Sunnah, and that the connection between the links of the chain to Muhammad ﷺ is like the link between the companions and Muhammad ﷺ and that, when he would tell the battalions, "Whoever obeys the commander has obeyed me and whoever disobeys the commander has disobeyed me", what do you think of the battalions of light marching to Allah, the most forgiving ﷻ?!

Their instructions are like the instructions of Muhammad ﷺ via the sheikhs among them who are nurturing and training them".

My teacher – may Allah be pleased with him – also said, "He who does not honour the sanctity of the one from whom he is learning manners will be deprived of the blessings of that education.

Therefore, whenever a person attains some knowledge or good etiquette but does not consider the status or honour of the one he learnt it from, will never benefit from that etiquette, good manners, and character or that knowledge. He will also never have an inkling of the true reality of that knowledge or etiquette even if he learns it outwardly because he has not honoured the one who taught it to him. This is why the pious people have said, 'Whoever asks his teacher 'why?' will never succeed, and they substantiated this with the following narration: 'If I have left something out, leave it alone... when I tell you something, take it from me. The reason those before you were destroyed is that they asked too many questions and they started arguing with their prophets''".

My teacher – may Allah be pleased with him – also said, "They asked Abu Mansūr al-Maghribi: 'How long were you in the company of Abu 'Uthmān?'

He replied: 'You mean; how long did I have the honour of serving him, not how long was I in his company. One accompanies one's brothers and peers. As for someone who is senior to me and far superior to me, I served him' – May Allah be pleased with him".

أدب أهل التصوف إنما أخذوه من الكتاب العزيز والسنة الغراء، وأن العلائق ما بين السند إلى محمد كالعلائق بين الصحب ومحمد صلَّى اللهُ وسلَّم وبارك عليه وعلى آله وصحبه، وأنه إن كان يقول لأهل السَّرايا «**من يطع الأمير.. فقد أطاعني، ومن عصى الأمير.. فقد عصاني**»، فكيف بسرايا النور إلى حضرة الغفور، إنما يكون أمرهم تبعٌ لأمره صلوات ربي وسلامه عليه عبر الشيوخ المربين فيهم.

وقال سيدي أيضاً: قال بعض المشائخ: **من لم يعظم حرمة من تأدب به.. حرم بركة ذلك الأدب.**

فهما أخذ من علم أو من أدب مع من لم يراع حرمته.. فإن ذلك الأدب والخلق وذلك العلم لا ينتفع به هو أبداً؛ ولا يعثر على حقيقة العلم ولا على حقيقة الأدب وإن أخذه؛ لأنه لم يعظم حرمة الذي أخذ منه هذا الأدب وحرمة الذي أخذ منه هذا العلم.

ولهذا قالوا:

من قال لأستاذه لِمَ.. لا يفلح أبداً. وأورد لنا الحديث: «اتركوني ما تركتكم، وإذا حدثتكم.. فخذوا عني، فإنما هلك من كان قبلكم.. بكثرة سؤالهم واختلافهم على أنبيائهم».

وقال سيدي أيضاً:

قالوا لأبي منصور المغربي: كم صحبت أبا عثمان؟ قال: خدمته لا صحبته؛ الصحبة مع الإخوان والأقران أما مع واحد أكبر مني وأرفع مني أنا خدمته، رضي اللهُ تعالى عنه.

A remedy for some objections a murīd may have regarding certain conditions of the sheikh

When a murīd has an objection or reservation regarding a certain condition of the sheikh, we mention the story of Mūsa ﷺ with Khadhir ﷺ because this is a perfect example with no transgression. It prevents the carnal self from the whisperings of the Devil, overthinking and falsely accusing the sheikh of something which he is not even sure is in the sheikh, and then deciding that the sheikh has transgressed the limits of the Sacred Law and can no longer be regarded as an example or benchmark because he disregarded a single etiquette – not a compulsory act and not that he did something haram!

The reason we sometimes see things that look like a contravention of the Sacred Law, but which are in fact not so at all, nor do they constitute disregard for any etiquettes whatsoever, is for the murīd to be tested and tried by Allah ﷻ and it is very similar to what transpired between the Followers (*Tābi'ūn*; the direct successors of the companions) and their successors. Many such tests and incidents happened to them.

Thus, we have to protect our internal selves; we have to protect our good thoughts of others. It is compulsory and binding upon us to consider the right of the pristine Sacred Law because it is applicable to both the people of outward practice as well as those who focus on the inner aspects. However, this applies when they are not clearly astray".

My teacher – may Allah be please with him – also said, "When Sayyidunā Junaid (Baghdadi) saw the resistance of some of those who attended his gatherings, he said, 'If you do not concur with me, then leave. You wanted to reach Allah and be connected to Him because of these things, so fulfil their rights and give them their due. If you do not want to, the world is vast and expansive – who forced you to come here to me?'"

How the murīd should be with the sheikh

My teacher – may Allah be pleased with him- also said, "The way a student and *murīd* should be whilst in the company of the sheikh... he should be ever so willing to serve him, be ready to receive spiritual bounties, and therefore it does not behove him to sit on a special carpet or even on his

معالجة استشكال المريد من بعض أحوال الشيخ:

إذا أشكل على المريد شيء -أي في حال الشيخ-.. يذكر قصة موسى مع الخضر، ففي هذا ميزان لا يطغى، وذلك أنه ينهى النفس عن الوسواس وحديث النفس والتهمة بما لا يوقَن فيه ويتعين خروجه عن الشرع، ثم لا يتخذ ذلك حجة للإخلال بأدب من آداب الشرع فضلاً عن واجب أو عن ارتكاب محرم.

وإنما قد تحضر صور لمخالفات لا مخالفة فيها في واقعها البتة، ولا خروج عن الأدب قيد أنملة؛ ولا قيد شعرة، ومع ذلك فيختبَرون بها اختباراً، ويمتحنون بها امتحاناً، فيكون ذلك كما هو واقع في قصصهم في تابع التابعين ومن بعدهم، وقع كثير من هذه الاختبارات ومن هذه القصص.

فوجب حفظ السر، وحفظ حسن الظن، ووجب مراعاة حق الشريعة الغراء فهي الحاكمة على أهل الظاهر وأهل الباطن كذلك، لكن من دون شطح لظاهر ومن دون رمي من صاحب باطن.

وقال سيدي أيضاً: ولما رأى المعارضة سيدنا الجنيد من بعض من يجلس معه، قال: إن لم تؤمنوا لي فاعتزلون، إنما أردتُّم الوصل والاتصال بهذه المعاني، فأعطوها حقها وقوموا بواجبها، وإلا فالأرض واسعة لكم، مَن الذي ألزمكم تجيؤون إلى عندنا.

وصف المريد عند الشيخ:

وقال سيدي أيضاً: وصف المريد والطالب عند الشيخ.. التبتل للخدمة، والتهيؤ لإفاضة النعمة، فلا يليق به أن يجلس على فرش مخصوص أو على سجادة بحضرة الشيخ.

prayer mat in the presence of the sheikh. Abu 'Abdillāh al-Suhrawardi ﷺ said, 'He should never lay his prayer mat on the ground in the presence of the sheikh unless it is time to pray. This is because part of being a student is being ever-ready to serve the sheikh and spreading out the prayer mat or sitting on it is an indication towards relaxation and the desire for being aloof. This means that he turns away from those around him, although this only behoves a person engaged in the remembrance of Allah in solitude, or even when he is in the presence of others. But he has no other obligations other than serving the sheikh or doing some kind of important task related to learning from the sheikh, spiritual advancement, or looking after the sheikh.

Look after the sheikh in all his conditions, perhaps
You will see some effect of this kindness upon you.

You know that this is how our masters the Noble Companions ﷺ treated our leader, Muhammad ﷺ the Chosen One. It was also the condition of the younger companions with the senior ones (though all of them are senior), and of the later companions with those who preceded them in faith – may Allah ﷻ be pleased with all of them. We also see that this was the behaviour of the Companions' successors and those who followed after them to such an extent that when they were mentioned in their absence, those who heard the speaker would start to feel a sense of honour and respect for them".

Being honest with the sheikhs

My teacher – may Allah be pleased with him – said, "Why do we want to be honest with the sheikhs? Because they are our door to Allah! Thus, we seek to achieve it through:

1. Sincere repentance
2. Complete abstention from all sin and wrongdoing.

This is because those who Allah ﷻ does not love, the sheikhs do not love him either".

He – may Allah be pleased with him – also said, "Which sheikh does

قال -أي أبو عبد الله السهروردي-: أن لا يبسط سجادته مع وجود الشيخ إلا لوقت الصلاة؛ فإن المريد من شأنه التبتل للخدمة، وفي السجادة إيماء إلى الاستراحة والتعزز؛ ومراده بالتعزز الإعراض عما حواليه، وإنما هذا يليق بحال الذاكر في خلوته أو في وقت حضوره مع خلوِّ جنابه من مطلوب خدمة وأداء مهمة تتعلق بالتلقي أو الترقي أو المراقبة لأحوال الشيخ.

وراقب الشيخ في أحواله فعسى   يرى عليك من استحسانه أثر

فعلمتَ ذلك من أحوال سادتنا الصحب رضي الله تعالى عنهم أمام المصطفى صلوات ربي وسلامه عليه، ثم أحوال صغار الصحابة مع كبارهم وكلهم كبير، ومتأخِّروا الصحابة مع سابقيهم وكلهم سابق عليهم رضوان الله تبارك وتعالى، ثم عُرف ذلك في شأن التابعين وتابع التابعين، حتى صار من خلال ذكرهم في غيبتهم يشعر من حواليهم بمعنى الإكبار والإجلال.

الصدق مع الشيوخ:

قال سيدي رضي الله عنه: لماذا نريد الصدق مع الشيوخ؛ لأنهم بابنا إلى الله، ولهذا نطلب ذلك:

١- بحسن التوبة.

٢- والإقلاع عن المعاصي والآثام؛ لأن الذي لا يحبه الله هم ما يحبونه.

وقال سيدي أيضاً: ما هو شيخ الذي لا يكره ما يكرهه الله، وكيف أنت تُصِر على شيء يكرهه الله وتقول: هذا شيخي.

not dislike what Allah ﷻ dislikes? So, how can you insist on doing that which Allah ﷻ dislikes, but you say: this is my sheikh!?"

Displaying good character to creation

My teacher – may Allah be please with him – said, "You have understood the wisdom of Allah ﷻ behind sending Messengers, revealing books, and the order in which He does things, even the angels. He engages with the creation with beautiful character. This is the secret behind giving the flag of praise to Muhammad ﷺ on the Day of Judgement.

Similarly, from the moment the beloved of Allah ﷺ left this world, his heirs were the cornerstones of helping the creation. They are on varying levels and of different statuses, the heights of which is called the Axis of the Time (*Quṭb al-Zamān*), the most perfect form of vicegerency.

They have reached incredible statuses. The brave men of this *ummah* have carried on with this from then until this very night and we are obliged to catch up with them.

The cure for one who thinks he knows, but he knows not

My teacher – may Allah be pleased with him – said, "We keep hinting and drawing your attention to certain things in many of our lectures and discourses, however some people are still blinded by the assumption that they understand the text, even though they make no progress. What has the text taught you if you make no progress? You have to understand the meaning of progress to begin with!

The one who has a spiritual connection, or who thinks he is a humble reformed person, we say to him: Humility and reformation is progress, so why have you stagnated? Or to the one who thinks he has submitted to Allah, we say: Submission is further progress, so why have you stagnated?

It is a very dangerous thing for a person to think that he has achieved.

This is our field... the field of neediness. Only those who have the attribute of neediness will tread this Path. Do not reject what they have for what you have when they direct you... do not let your perception become a barrier.

التجلي على الخلق بالخلق:

قال سيدي رَضِيَ اللهُ عَنْهُ: قد علمتم حكمة الحق في إرسال الرسل وإنزال الكتب وفي ترتيب حتى الملائكة، إنما يتجلّى على الخلق بالخلق هذا سر حمل اللواء في القيامة.

كذلكم ما لحظة مرّت من بعد أن فارق حبيب الله العالم إلاّ وورّاثه أساس إمداد الخلق، وهم في ذلك على مراتب ينتهون إلى قطب الزمان وكامل الخلافة في الشأن.

ما أعجب مراتبهم؛ على هذا مضى رجال الأمة إلى ليلتكم هذه التي أنتم فيها فيجب أن تدركوا.

علاج من يظن أنه يدري وهو لا يدري:

قال سيدي رَضِيَ اللهُ عَنْهُ: نحن نكثر الإشارة في كثير من الكلام والتنبيه، ولكن بعض كلاليب الناس هذه تحجبهم يظن أنه عرف العبارة لكنه ما ترقى، وما دلالة العبارة إن لم يترقَّ بها، لا بد من معرفة معنى الترقي.

من كان صاحب انتساب أو يظن أنه صاحب انكسار نقول له: الانكسار ترقي فلماذا وقفت؟ أو يظن أنه صاحب تسليم فنقول: التسليم زيادة لماذا وقفت؟ هذا أمر خطير أن يظن الإنسان أنه أدرك.

ميداننا هذا.. ميدان الفقر، لا يسلك فيه إلاّ من اتصف بالفقر، لا تَرُد ما عندهم بما عندك إذا أشاروا، فلا تجعل فكرك يحجبك.

فإن تركت ما عندك.. أعطوك ما عندهم؛ وإن تشبّثت بما عندك.. حجبت به، المرء من حيث قلبه.

If you abandon what you have... they will give you what they have. If you cling to what you have, you will be blinded by it. A man is what is in his heart. This is why our teacher, Sheikh Abu Bakr bin Sālim ﷺ, used to say, "As long as you live, just stay at our door".

The vastest door of mercy

My teacher – may Allah be pleased with him – said, "This is why one of the vastest doors of mercy is the door of salutations upon the Messenger of Allah ﷺ. The murīd should try to envision the blessed Prophet ﷺ when sending salutations. Otherwise, he can envision the sheikh he is affiliated to, or the pious people".

"No matter what level you are on, if you wish to enter into the Divine Presence from anywhere other than the door, Allah ﷻ will not accept you. Even the Prophet ﷺ will not accept you unless you show the proper etiquette and you stand at the right door. This is just how Allah ﷻ does things. You want to transgress the rights due to others and then still hope to reach Allah... is this a joke?!

This is servitude to Allah. We do not seek that which Allah ﷻ has prohibited; we do not seek prohibited things with that which Allah ﷻ has given us, nor do we seek what He has given by means of what He has prohibited.

Proof that "Spiritual Doctors" (sheikhs) have been around since the time of the Prophet ﷺ as well as a description of the murīds

My teacher – may Allah be pleased with him – said, "From the time of the Beloved of Allah ﷺ, there has never been a time in which there were no spiritual doctors (i.e. sheikhs). We have not inherited nothing... we have inherited sheikhs who take care of us – may Allah be pleased with them. Allah ﷻ has an army of such people whom He specially selected. It is not an easy task to be enlisted in the army of Allah!

He ﷻ has prepared the greatest means (of gaining proximity) for us throughout the ages. No one can find something like it and this has

لهذا قال سيدنا الشيخ أبو بكر بن سالم: **(واجعل وقوفك ما بقيت ببانا).**

أوسع أبواب الرحمة:

قال سيدي رَضِيَ اللهُ عَنْهُ: وهذا **كان من أوسع أبواب الرحمة.. الصلاة على النبي صلَّى الله عليه وآله وصحبه وسلَّم، فيتخيّلوا صورته الشريفة أو يتخيل صورة شيخه المنسوب إليه ورجال الحق.**

مهما كان الواحد في أي درجة وأردت أن تدخل عليه من غير الباب.. ما يقبلك، حتى النبي صلَّى الله عليه وآله وصحبه وسلَّم لا يقبلك من غير أدبك ووقوفك على أبوابه؛ لأنه ترتيب الحق كذا، أنت تريد تتعدى الحقوق وتصل، هل هذه ضحكه؟!

هذه عبودية لله ما نطلب الأشياء من حيث المنع، ولا نطلب المنع من حيث أعطى، أو عطاء من حيث مَنَعَ.

وجود المداوين من عهد النبي صَلَّى اللهُ عَلَيْهِ وَسَلَّمَ، مع ذكر أوصاف المريدين:

قال سيدي رَضِيَ اللهُ عَنْهُ:

ما أُعدم المداوون من يوم جاء الحبيب محمد صلَّى الله عليه وآله وصحبه وسلَّم، ما حصَّلْنا جفا، حصَّلْنا شيوخ يدلّعونا عليهم رضوان الله، ولله في البرية جنود اختارهم هو، و لا هو سهل الدخول في جندية للرب.

هيّأ لكم أسباب عظيمة على مدى العصور، ما أحد يجد مثلها كما كان المريدون يُختبرون ويبتلون ابتلاء، فتهيأت هكذا لنا الأسباب فعلينا نتنبه، نعرف معنى الترقي وزيادته، لا تقنع بحالك، لا تجعل الركب يمشي وأنت قاعد.

been the experience of the *murīds* time and time again. We also have these means and avenues, so we have to be attentive and understand the meaning of progress and what comes beyond. Never become complacent with your current condition! Do not let the caravan move on whilst you remain seated!

May Allah grant all of us the inspiration not to stagnate at any part of our journey – not our deeds, not our intellect, and not our spiritual conditions. *Inshā'Allāh*, if we inculcate this, we will be engulfed in Divine Grace and we will be freed from the shackles and chains into a lofty station – the One we call out to and who responds, the True, the One who answers, our Lord who is ever so near!"

My teacher – may Allah be pleased with him – also said, "All praise is due to Allah for blessing us with compassionate sheikhs and pure mercy. Had He not made them compassionate and they had to test us... O Allah, Concealer of faults! Habib Aḥmad bin Ḥasan al-'Aṭṭās used to say, 'We would go to the door of Habib Aḥmad bin Ḥasan al-'Aṭṭās and he would ignore us from early morning until the afternoon – knowing full well that we are there, standing in the sun – but he would not even speak to us until he would open the door for me. However, I would still not leave. Today, if someone comes to our door at home and knocks but hears no answer, he turns away and leaves. Actually, he was just looking for an excuse so that he can say: no one answered; there was no one there.

People have different aspirations, different levels of perseverance, and different goals. Those who are true in their quest will be enveloped in Divine Grace and a truly yearning soul will be recognised.

O Allah! Grant us the divine inspiration to put these words into practice until we breath our last, and meet with You at last!'"

My teacher – may Allah be pleased with him – also said, "A similar incident is related about Imam 'Ali bin 'Abdullah al-Saqqāf who went to his sheikh, 'Abdullah bin 'Alawi al-Aydarūs in India when the sheikh was in India. He said, 'Leave him (i.e. Imam 'Ali bin 'Abdullah al-Saqqāf) by the door'. And so they left him. Other people came too and they were given permission to enter, one after the other while Imam 'Ali remained at the door. This continued until everyone else had entered and they were all seated, and the gathering was bustling... and he was still outside at the

الله يوفقنا وإياكم، ما نقف عند شيء من أعمالنا وعقولنا وأحوالنا أبداً إن شاء الله، فتحيط بنا العناية ونتخلص من القيد والحصر بعد ذلك إلى الأوج الفسيح، **نريد الملبي المجيب والصادق المستجيب وربنا أقرب قريب.**

وقال سيدي أيضاً:

الحمد لله الذي أكرمنا بشيوخ حنان ورحمه خالصة، وإلا لو امتحنونا كان يا ستّار، الحبيب أحمد بن حسن العطاس يقول: نأتي على باب الحبيب أبي بكر العطاس فيتركنا من الصبح إلى الظهر وهو يعلم بي في الشمس ولا يكلمنا حتى يفتح لي بعد ذلك، ولكن لا أنصرف، والآن إذا جاء ودق الباب على دارنا وما أحد كلّمه ذهب، أصلاً هو يريد العذر، فيقول: ما أحد كلمنا، ما حصلت أحد.

العزائم.. تختلف، والهمم.. تختلف، والمقاصد.. تختلف، والرعاية بالصادق.. تكتنف، وروح المقبل.. تعترف.

فإن قالوا: انصرف، قال:

إن أحمد اسم لا ينصرف، فإن قال: أنا شاعر أصرف ما لا ينصرف، قيل له: صرفك يحول النحاس ذهباً فتصرّف كما شئت، فقد علِمنا شغل الصيارفة، يا الله بالتوفيق حتى نفيق ونلحق بالفريق.

وقال سيدي أيضاً:

وهكذا جاء أيضاً الإمام علي بن عبد الله السقاف إلى شيخه عبد الله بن علي العيدروس في الهند لما كان في الهند، فقال:

اتركوه على الباب، وتركوه، ودخل الناس يؤذن لواحد بعد الثاني وهو على الباب

door. Supper was presented to them and they all ate, all the while Imam 'Ali remained at the door without moving or turning away.

After supper, Sheikh 'Abdullah bin 'Alawi al-Aydarūs ﷺ: 'Go see if the sheikh is still at the door or if he has left'. When they returned, they said, 'He is still at the door, the way he was when we arrived'. He replied, 'Take this water that the people have washed their hands in and pour it over his head'. And so, they took the dirty water that the guests had washed their hands in and poured it over his head. When he was drenched, he said, 'The leftovers from the home of my sheikh' and started wiping it all over himself. 'What did he say?' asked the sheikh. 'He said it was the blessings from the home of his sheikh and started rubbing it all over himself' they replied.

'Let him in!' he said. And they did... but now the veil was lifted, his position was elevated, and he achieved proximity along with those who had achieved it, and he was honoured with a special glance which resulted in him leaving as one of the attendees. This happened only after his sincerity in his quest had been perfected, his precedence proven, and he did not get affected at all by what had transpired.

So many sheikhs tested their *murīds* in a similar way. Habib Aḥmad bin Ḥasan al-'Aṭṭās ﷺ said, 'Nowadays, if someone comes and knocks on the door for a short time, or he calls out and no-one responds, he leaves because he actually just wants an excuse. He has no real interest or sincerity in this path'".

He also said, "Some of the sheikhs of Makkah used to be the same way. They would say, 'You came with a lofty (*'alawī*) aura about you like a hat on your head (i.e. thinking you're special). When you take it off, I'll let you in'.

Another similar incident is reported regarding some students who came to Habib 'Ali al-Mashhūr ﷺ. He said, 'Before you recite anything to me, go to the market and buy the following: x, y and z and also some meat'. The student said, 'No problem, but do you have a container or a basket?'. 'What! A container or a basket?!

What's wrong with your sleeves? They are so large you could very easily fit everything I have asked you to buy in them'. The student left and returned with everything the sheikh had asked for and, on top of that, it

حتى تكامل الناس وجلسوا، وطاب مجلسهم، وهو على الباب، وقُدِّم لهم الغداء وتغدَّوا، وهو على الباب واقف لا ينصرف ولا يتحرك.

فقال بعد الغداء: انظروا هل هذا السيد لا يزال على الباب أو ذهب؟

رجعوا فقالوا: واقف على الباب كحاله من حين جاء، قال: خذوا هذا الغسل حق أيدي الناس وصبوه فوق رأسه، وأخذوا الغُسالة التي غسلوا بها الناس صبوها فوق رأسه، ولما وصلت قال: هذا أثر من آثار بيت شيخي فأخذ يتمسح به، ماذا قال؟

قالوا: قال: بركات شيخي وتمسح بها، قال: افتحوا له الباب، ففتحوا الباب وانزاح الحجاب وارتفعت الرتب وحصل القربة مع من قرب وأُكرم بنظرة خرج فيها وهو من أهل الحضرة، لما تكامل صدقه وحَقَّ سبقه ولم يتأثر من هذا.

وهكذا كم اختبروا الشيوخ تلامذتهم بمثل ذلك، قال الحبيب أحمد بن حسن العطاس: والآن إذا جاء واحد ودق الباب قليل أو نادى ولا أحد سمعه ذهب؛ لكونه يريد العذر وما له رغبة ولا له صدق في الوجهة.

وهكذا قال:

كان بعض مشائخ مكة كذلك، ثم قال له: إنما جئت ومعك شَمْخَة عَلَوية فوق رأسك، فلما نزَّلتها.. فتحنا لك.

وهكذا جاء بعضهم لطلب العلم أيضاً من الحبيب عبد الرحمن المشهور، فيقول: قبل القراءة أو الدرس أول اذهب هات الحاجة الفلانية من السوق، اشتر لنا كذا وكذا -ومن جملته- وهات لحم، فيقول: مرحباً عندكم وعاء أو زنبيل، فيقول: وعاء وزنبيل!! ماذا بكمّك؟!

was all in his sleeves.

Then the Sheikh said, 'Now you may be seated and recite to me, no problem. You have now prepared yourself and you are worthy of reciting to me'.

SubhānAllah!

Ibn 'Abbās ﵄ said that he used to stand at the door of his sheikh, Zaid bin Thābit ﵁ for an hour, two hours, three hours, sometimes four and sometimes from the early morning until midday. He did not like to knock on his door because he did not want to disturb him, but at the same time, he did not want to leave either.

He would remain at his sheikh's door even when, at times, the wind would pick up and blow dust around and he would be covered in dust to the extent that you could not see who he was! People would walk past him and not know who he is because he was so dirty, but still he would not leave until Zaid ﵁ himself noticed him there.

He said, "O Ibn 'Abbās! I am embarrassed by you doing this because of your close relationship and familial ties to the Prophet ﷺ so, please, do not just come. Rather, let me know beforehand when I can expect you". But he ﵁ kept on doing this.

A sign of being connected to Allah

My teacher – may Allah ﷻ be pleased with him – said, "When this is complete, you will be honoured with a connection to Allah.

It is the system of Allah that, when He wants someone to be connected to Him, He connects that person to someone He loves. His connection to this friend (walī) of Allah prepares him for a connection with the greatest Imam (Muhammad ﷺ) and when this is complete... he reaches Allah!

Therefore, if a person does not want to connect himself to someone who Allah ﷻ loves (in other words, the friends of Allah)... do not be fooled by what he says and does.

He will never reach Allah even if he fills the Earth with worship.

كمّك كبير يصلح فيه تحطه في الكم حقك، فخرج وجاء وأحضر الحاجة وجابها، والزائد حَطَّهُ في كمِّه، قال: الآن اجلس، ستقرأ لا بأس، بدأت تتهيأ وتصلح للقراءة، سبحان الله!!

قال ابن عباس:

كان يقف على باب شيخه سيدنا زيد بن ثابت عليهم رضوان الله الساعة والساعتين والثلاث والأربع الساعات قد يقف من أول النهار إلى الظهر على باب شيخه، لا يرضى أن يطرق الباب خشية أن يزعجه ولا يريد أن ينصرف، حتى قد تهب الريح بالغبار فيمتلئ غباراً إلى حدّ أن لا يُميَّز في بعض الأحيان، فيمر المار لا يعرف مَن هذا مِن كثرة الغبار الذي عليه وهو لا يريد أن ينصرف، حتى شعُر به زيد وقال: يا ابن عباس إني أستحي من رسول الله صلَّى الله عليه وسلَّم وقرابتك منه، فلا تأتي إلى الباب ولكن أشعرني من قبل أن تجيء، ولم يزل بهذا الحال.

من علامات الجمعية على الحق تعالى:

قال سيدي رَضِيَ اللهُ عَنْهُ:

فإذا تمَّ هذا.. أُكرمت بالجمعية.

من عادة الحق إذا أراد يجمع عليه أحد.. جمعه على محبوب، فيهيئه الجمع على ذلك المحبوب.. بالاجتماع بالإمام الأعظم، فإذا تمَّ الاجتماع عليه.. وصل إلى باريه.

وإذا ما أراد يجمع إنسان عليه.. فلا يغرُّك ما يكرره من كلام ولا ما يفعله من أفعال، فلن يصل ولو ملأ الأرض عبادة.

Proximity is dependent on being annihilated in Muhammad ﷺ

My teacher – may Allah be pleased with him – said, "Respected brothers! Know that their statuses and positions (in terms of proximity to Allah) depended on how much they had become like Muhammad. There is nothing without this. How else do you think you will gain proximity to Allah?

The same principle applied to all those who came after them until this very night – your proximity is proportionate to how much you annihilate yourself in the sheikh. Many people are delusional about their level of proximity, but there is no resemblance between them and their sheikh. Is it possible for an airplane to take you up into the sky when you have not even boarded it to begin with? Can it happen if you are sitting outside the airplane saying: 'I'm going to fly in an airplane'?

InshāAllah we will become like Muhammad! Habib 'Ali made the following prayer: 'O Allah! Send such salutations upon our master, Muhammad, that please you and please him and that make my every action and inaction just like his'".

Love for the sheikh

My teacher – may Allah be pleased with him – said, "Those who believe in the sheikh are many, but there are very few who love him. Love does not just mean an inclination or respect.

You will develop love when you truly and deeply understand that he (the sheikh) is a favour of Allah and a door to get to Him ﷻ*. In this way, love will become something significant, something that keeps growing and it becomes a kind of love for Allah* ﷻ *Himself.* Amazingly, this is alluded to in the magnificent and holy hadith of the Prophet ﷺ (and I am paraphrasing): He who loves someone for the sake of Allah, he who visits his brother for the sake of Allah—my love becomes compulsory for those who love each other for my sake – in other words, because of love for Allah".

The Prophetic tree

The tree of Mūsa ﷺ was a plant. We also have the trees of the Prophet

القرب على قدر الانطواء:

قال سيدي رضي الله عنه: الصحب الكرام اعلم أن مراتبهم.. على قدر انطوائهم في **محمد**، غير هذا لا يوجد، من أين أحدهم سيأتي بالقرب؟! واستمرت لمن بعدهم، **فقربه.. على قدر انطوائه في شيخه** إلى ليلتنا هذه.

كثير من الناس تخيّلوا خيالات والانطواء لا يوجد، هل يمكن ترتفع بك الطائرة وأنت ما دخلت وسطها؟! جالس في الخارج وتقول: أنا سأطير بالطائرة.

إن شاء الله ننطوي، قال الحبيب علي: (**اللهم صلِّ على سيدنا محمد صلاة ترضيك وترضيه وتنطوي جميع حركاتي وسكناتي فيه**).

محبة الشيخ:

قال سيدي رضي الله عنه: الذين يعتقدون في الشيوخ كثير والذين يحبونهم قليل، المحبة لا بمجرد الميل ولا بمجرد التعظيم.

وتأتي المحبة من انغراس معنى إدراك أنه منّة من الله، وأنه الباب إليه، فتصير المحبة فيها معنى راقي سامي ترجع إلى الجزء من محبة الذات العلية؛ لأن محبة الذات العلية يترتب عليها ولأجلها.

والعجب جاء التعبير في الأحاديث القدسية والنبوية (بفيَّ)، أنه يحبه في الله، من زار أخاً في الله، وجبت محبتي للمتحابين فيَّ.

الشجرة النبوية:

قال سيدي رضي الله عنه: شجرة سيدنا موسى الكليم.. من نوع النباتات، وعندنا

of Allah ﷺ but they are not plants.

Rather, they are in the form of people. Therefore, it is only fitting for these trees to be the mirrors of Divine Manifestation (O Allah! Send Your salutations upon Muhammad, the original tree of light ﷺ)".

How things are perfected in our field

My teacher – may Allah be pleased with him – said, "In our filed (spiritual reformation), perfection is attained through:

1. Discipline in terms of true allegiance to Allah ﷻ through faith.
2. Being learned with the correct beliefs ('Aqeedah).
3. Being learned with understanding – in other words, with intelligence, wisdom, and a certain level of clarity regarding the fact that we have a deep concern for good character, treading the path, the path itself, and knowledge.

Proportionate to the level of their faith... they will attain steadfastness, they will be divinely selected, they will be pleased with their Lord and they will be entered into the ranks of His divine army".

The attributes of a Reviver (Awakener)

My teacher – may Allah be pleased with him – said, "Every reviver [someone who wakes others up from the slumber of their heedlessness] truly feels like he has a duty, a responsibility, that he has to call others towards Him [Allah], and that he has a small connection to the prophetic light of guidance. He has a deep concern for Him [Allah]... he has a worry and a concern that takes over his entire heart.

This practice is something that Allah ﷻ has only given to His Prophets and those who believed in them. He ﷻ has given this responsibility to us.

All praise is due to Allah ﷻ who has given us the responsibility of His most beloved. Furthermore, He has honoured us and you by making our authentic chain that leads up to him ﷺ and the rope that ties us to him one of the strongest and most encompassing ropes and chains. It comprises great scholars who narrate from great scholars!

One of us enters this chain dirty and full of faults, but leaves having

أشجار محمد وهي ليست من نوع النباتات، بل نوع الإنسان نفسه، فجدير بأن تكون مرآة للتجلي، (اللهم صلِّ على سيدنا محمد شجرة الأصل النورانية).

إتمام الأمور في مجالنا:

قال سيدي رضي الله عنه: تتم الأمور في مجالنا:

١- بانضباط من جهة الولاء الخالص لله بالإيمان.

٢- ويؤخذ الأمر عن عقيدة.

٣- ومع تدرّج بمعنى العقلية والحكمة بشيء من الوضوح أن عندنا هَمْ بجانب الأخلاق والسير والطريق والعلم.

على حسب إيمانهم.. يحصل لهم الثبات، ويطلعون في الانتخابات، ويرتضون من الرب، ويقعون من جنده.

أوصاف المتنبِّه:

قال سيدي رضي الله عنه: كل متنبّه شعر أن عليه واجب، عليه مسؤولية، وأن عليه دعوة، وأن له صله بالنور المحمدي له رابطة جزئية فيه، له هَمٌّ به، له أمر يهمه يأخذ بمجامع قلبه. هذا العمل جعله الله للأنبياء و لأتباعهم المؤمنين فقط، ووكلها إلينا. الحمد لله الذي وكل إلينا أعمال حبيبه المجتبى، ثم تكرّم علينا وعليكم بأن جعل سندنا إليه والحبال التي تربطنا به من أقوى وأوسع الحبال والأسانيد، كبار عن كبار، يخرج الواحد منا بوسخه وما فيه من عيوب.. فيطلع في السجل تبع الأقطاب الكبار.

been cleansed completely with his name written as a follower of the greatest scholars".

The connection to the Beloved of Allah ﷺ

My teacher – may Allah be pleased with him – said, "A connection to the Beloved of Allah ﷺ who brought us the message from Allah ﷻ is a connection of the heart, a connection of the soul, with those who have accepted this divine message as exemplified and personified in the being of Muhammad ﷺ. This connection of acceptance is a connection between them and the Lord of the Heavens and the Earth, by means of which they will be elevated in this world and the next in rank, honour, and status.

This connection with every single believer in the Heavens and the Earth is very special and different. It is the most noble connection... a connection of those very special people in the *ummah* who have entered into the fold of our master Muhammad ﷺ and who resemble him. This distinctive feature sets them apart from all the previous nations as well as all those who preceded them of all creation who had some connection to the singularity and oneness of Allah and who had some kind of faith in the King of Kings, the Lord of the Worlds.

However, O *ummah* of Muhammad, our connection has a special strength because it is attributed to the final Prophet ﷺ and, so, we thank Allah ﷻ for this distinction and speciality!

Reaching the pious

My teacher – may Allah be pleased with him – said, "Many people sit in the gatherings and company of the pious but they never actually reach them. On the other hand, many know them and have reached them. There are also many who fit into both the aforementioned categories and, in so doing, get the value of both and achieve both types of good fortune.

They are present both in person and in heart, they are close both physically and in spirit, they see with both their eyes and with their insight... they are recognised and so they achieve the recognition of Allah; they are taken in by the sheikhs and, so, they reach Allah. Do not ask about their

النسبة إلى حبيب الرحمن:

قال سيدي رضي الله عنه: النسبة إلى حبيب الرحمن الذي جاءت به الرسالة.. نسبة قلبية ونسبة روحية، مع أهل دائرة الاستجابة لهذه الرسالة السماوية المتمثلة في الحضرة المحمدية، وكانت نسبة هذه الاستجابة نسبة بينهم وبين رب الأرض والسماء يعلي لهم بها الشأن هنا وهناك فضلاً وكرماً.

وهذه النسبة مع كل مؤمن من المؤمنين من أهل الأرض والسماء.. تميزت واختلفت، فكان أشرف النسب.. نسبة المنطويين في دائرة سيدنا محمد صلَّى الله عليه وآله وصحبه وسلَّم من خصوص أمته، فكانت لهم بهذه الخصوصية تَمَيُّز عن الأمم السابقة، وتَمَيُّز عمن قبلهم من أنواع الخلائق الذين كانت معهم نسبة التوحيد ونسبة الإيمان بالملك المجيد.

غير أننا معشر الأمة كان لنسبتنا قوة من حيث انتماءنا لخاتم النبوة صلَّى الله عليه وآله وصحبه وسلَّم؛ فالحمد لله على هذه الميزة وهذه الخصوصية.

الوصول إلى الأولياء:

قال سيدي رضي الله عنه:

كثير من الناس جالسوا الأولياء ولا وصلوا إليهم، وكثير عرفوهم ووصلوا إليهم، وكثير ممن جمع بين المقامين، وأخذ بالطرفين، ونال السعادتين، وحضر بالجسم والقلب، وقرب بالشبح والروح، ونظر بالبصر والبصيرة، **فعُرِّف.. فعرف، وأوصل.. فوصل، وبعد ذلك عن حاله.. فلا تسل**، فإنه (لا يعرف الشوق.. إلا من يكابده، ولا الصبابة.. إلا من يعانيها).

condition after that because:

Only those willing to make the sacrifice
Will understand the pleasure of desire.
Only those willing to bear the burden
Of love will ever really attain it.

Thus, explaining that condition and state to those who have not attained it is like explaining impossibilities to people who minds are unable to even imagine its existence. It is also like explaining the intricacies of being a king and the enjoyments of the kingdom to a small child with a limited intellect.

Glory be to the One who opens the door of His generosity to those who call out to Him. All praise is due to Him, the Glorious and Exalted!

The history of spiritual gatherings

My teacher – may Allah be pleased with him – said, "These gatherings of ours... it is also a practice which we have inherited from our predecessors and Allah ﷻ has made it a solid link in a chain that links us to those great luminaries. The realities which are discussed and taught in these gatherings... their source is those magnificent gatherings which, in turn, got their effulgence from that magnificent being seated among them, sitting there among them in spirit, wherever they were. It is a spirit and soul, the vastness, nobility, manifestness, and blessedness of which the entire universe has never witnessed... it is the spirit of Muhammad ﷺ, the Chosen One."

Recognising one's vicegerency through intuition and expression

My teacher – may Allah be pleased with him – said, "The way we realise that we have reached the stage of vicegerency is through intuition and expression. Realising it through intuition is what removes the spiritual ailments of the heart and realising it through expression removes the spiritual deficiencies in one's deeds.

فإنّ وصف ذلك الحال لمن لم يبلغه.. كوصف المحالات عند بعض العقول التي تفكر فيها فلا تتصور وجودها، وهي أيضاً كمن يصف شؤون السلطة وملذة الملك لصبي غير مميز.

سبحانه فاتح أبواب جوده لمن استسداه، فله الحمد سبحانه وتعالى!!

سلسلة المجالس:

قال سيدي رضي الله عنه:

إنّ مجالسنا هذه.. إنما هي سلسلة من تلك السلاسل، جعلها الله حلقة محكمة مربوطة بأولئك القوم، وحقائق ما في المجلس.. إنما كان معدنها تلك المجالس، ومعدنها.. ذلكم الجالس بين أظهرهم، وهو الجالس بروحه بين أحبابه حيثما كانوا وأينما كانوا، وهي الروح التي ما شهدت الأكوان أوسع منها، ولا أكرم منها، ولا أظهر منها، ولا أبرك منها روح محمد المختار صلَّى الله وسلَّم عليه وعلى آله.

استشعار النيابة بالذوق والترجمة:

قال سيدي رضي الله عنه:

مجال استشعار النيابة عندكم.. بالذوق والترجمة، أما استشعاره بالذوق.. ينهي على القلب، واستشعاره بالترجمة.. ينهي على الأعمال.

ولولا الفوائد الكبرى في شأن الارتباط بالنيابة الذوقي والعملي، والمترجم عنه بما قال صلَّى الله عليه وسلَّم «**بلِّغوا عني ولو آية**».. لما دعينا إليه.

لذا أي وقت تريد أن تبلغ.. يكون لك حبل موصل إلى النبي، وباب يدخلك عليه،

If there was no benefit to this spiritual connection through vicegerency in the form of intuition and expression – as is represented by the words of the Prophet ﷺ "Convey what you have learnt from me even if it is a single verse..." – we would not have been called towards it.

Therefore, whenever you wish to reach... you will have a strong rope that joins you to the Prophet ﷺ, a door by means of which you would be able to enter upon him ﷺ and you will then be able to reach a position that has been authentically transmitted from him ﷺ. However, if you come with your own intellect, your own ideas, and your own carnal self... then these doors are not meant for you, nor will entering these doors be of any assistance to you in reaching your desired destination.

When you cut out this vicegerency... spiritual ailments will envelope the heart and spiritual decay will ravage the deeds. This is why it is a great blessing and favour of Allah ﷻ that we have a spiritual connection that is validated by a chain of transmission. Therefore, the sheikh will let the murīd reach [vicegerency] because he has the connection, the door, the rope... and he will realise this vicegerency.

He will experience it through his intuition and he will thus be cured of conceit and self-absorption and his heart will be freed from harbouring jealousy and malice or from inclining towards immoral behaviour. He will realise it and express it through his good deeds by purifying them of deficiencies and shortcomings.

By realising vicegerency through intuition
The ailments of the heart are gone.
By realising vicegerency through expression
Purity of deeds is won.

The one who becomes a link in the chain of succession and vicegerency which is linked to prophethood... should fear Allah with regards to his intuition and his expression. The more true and honest he is in this, he will achieve magnificent things and attributes of procrastination, heedlessness, laziness, and complacency will fade into oblivion. This is because the carnal is self-inclined towards rest and relaxation, and towards fulfilling its desires, etc."

فتبلغ بلاغاً صحيحاً عنه، وإن جئت معك عقل أو فكر أو نفس.. فهذه ليست بأبواب تدخلك عليه، وليست بأبواب توصلك إليه.

إذا انقطعت النيابة.. حلّت العلل في القلب والعلل في العمل.

فلهذا كان من نعمة الله.. الارتباط بالسند وربط الحبال، فيبلِّغ المبلِّغ ومعه رابطة، ومعه باب، ومعه حبل، فيستشعر هذه النيابة.

يستشعرها بالذوق.. فيذهب عنه العجب والغرور، ويربو بقلبه عن أن يحسد أو يحقد أو يلتفت إلى الدنايا، ويستشعرها ويترجمها في حسن أعماله.. بما يصلحها وينقيها عن الخلل.

باستشعار النيابة ذوقاً.. تذهب علل القلوب.

وباستشعار النيابة ترجمة.. تذهب علل الأعمال.

ومن كان ينوب عن حبال النيابة المتصلة بالنبوة.. فليتق الله في ذوقه وترجمته، وهو بذلك مهما صَدَقَ.. يتهيأ إلى شيء كبير، وتتلاشى منه أوصاف الإهمال والإغفال والتكاسل وركون النفس، فالنفس تركن إلى الراحة وإلى الدعة وإلى الالتفات إلى شهواتها وما إلى ذلك.

What we need to focus on and prepare for – a message to those who call others towards righteousness

My teacher – may Allah be pleased with him – said, "We really have to think about the following things carefully and prepare for them properly:

1. Understanding Allah, the Subtle, The All-Knowing ﷻ.
2. Ascending the levels of proximity to Him ﷻ.
3. Endearing ourselves to Him ﷻ.
4. Standing at the door.
5. Knocking at the doors from the front.
6. Choosing the most expansive door.

This is why I would like to draw the attention of those calling to righteousness to the following

1. Making a serious and concerted effort to purify and cleanse their inner selves.
2. Establishing these attributes within themselves such that they desire progress every moment of the day and night and are not heedless and unmindful of it for a second, and that they make their preparations and effort. This is what we call "Annihilation in the Sheikh" (becoming carbon copies of the sheikh).
3. Teaching them to deny their own self which is being purified, cleansed, spiritually nurtured and made pleasing to Allah.... And that, without denying the self, one's submission will be incomplete as long as the self is there.

It is like a person who goes to someone who washes clothes and says, 'Here are my clothes and I would like you to wash them', however, he is wearing them and walking around with them and refuses to take them off. The person will ask, 'Are you playing the fool with me? Why are you wearing the clothes if you really want me to wash them for you? I you truly want me to wash them, then give me your clothes. We have other clothes to wash and we will wash your clothes at the same time. In fact, we will even fold them for you when we are done!'

جوانب التفكير والتشمير، والتنبيه للدعاة:

قال سيدي رَضِيَ اللهُ عَنْهُ: نحتاج إلى كثير من التفكير والتشمير في جانب:

١- الفهم عن اللطيف الخبير.

٢- وارتقاء درجات القرب إليه.

٣- والتحبب لديه.

٤- والوقوف على الباب.

٥- وطرق الأبواب على وجهها.

٦- واختيار الأوسع منها.

من أجل أن يتنبه الدعاة إلى:

١- قوة الجهد في تصفية البواطن، وتنقية السرائر.

٢- وتقويم الصفات فيهم، بحيث يطلبون الرقي بعد ذلك في كل أيامهم ولياليهم، بحيث لا يغفلون عنه فيأخذون عدته، وهي الانطواء في المشايخ.

٣- وتعلّم إنكار الذات التي تتطهر وتتنظف وتتزكى وتُرتضى؛ وأنه دون إنكارها.. لا يصح تسليمها ما دامت ذاتك معك موجودة.

فإن كنت تعرف أن تطهِّر.. طهِّرها، لكن إذا سلمتها.. فالمسلَّمة أولى بتطهيرها وتنقيتها. كالذي يقف على المنظِّف والمغسِّل ويقول له: هذه ثيابي أريد منك غَسْلها، ويمشي بها معه، أو يكون لابساً لها ولا يريد إخراجها، ويمر كل يوم على المغسِّل

The effect of making the effort and submitting

My teacher – may Allah be pleased with him – said, "You need both – to make the effort and to submit.

The one who makes effort but does not submit
Will ultimately end in destruction.
The one who submits but makes no effort
Will never reach his destination.

Therefore, you have to have both submission and effort in the sense that you do good deeds, exert yourself, work hard, ponder, abandon your own opinion... and you must be submissive, pleased with your circumstances, at peace, and obedient. That is where success lies!"

How to be connected to the Prophet ﷺ

My teacher – may Allah be pleased with him – said, "People's affairs will fall into place proportionate to these connections. One can never attain a connection to the Prophet ﷺ without establishing a connection with his successors and vicegerents. In every era, the path to a connection with Muhammad, the Chosen One ﷺ, is via the representatives of that era. This is the system of Allah ﷻ.

The connected person

My teacher said, "You will find a connected person to be such that all his matters are in order, a little of what he does will be superior to a great deal of effort from anyone else, and the little he gives will have far more blessings and will have a far greater effect".

A person with a weak connection

My teacher – may Allah be pleased with him – said, "A person with a weak connection... is like someone who boasts about outwards displays that have no real substance; he will be of the view that he is independent

ويقول له: غسِّل ثيابي، يقول له المغسِّل: هل أنت تستهزئ؟ فماذا الآن أنت لابس؟ إذا أردت مني غَسْلها بصدق.. فأعطني ملابسك، فمعنا المغاسل التي تنظف، سننظفها لك، بل وسنكويها بعد ذلك، وهكذا.

شأن الإقدام والاستسلام:

قال سيدي رَضِيَ اللَّهُ عَنْهُ: لا بد من إقدام واستسلام.

فصاحب الإقدام بلا استسلام.. أمره إلى انهدام.

وصاحب الاستسلام بلا إقدام.. يفوّت المرام.

فلا بد من استسلام وإقدام، بحيث تعمل وتجتهد وتبذل وتفكر وتضع الرأي.. وأنت مستسلم راضٍ مطمئن منقاد، فهناك النجح.

كيفية الرابطة بالنبي ﷺ:

قال سيدي رَضِيَ اللَّهُ عَنْهُ: إنما تنضبط أمور الناس.. بحسب هذه الروابط.

الرابطة بنبيه ورسوله.. لا تأتي بدون رابطة بخلفائه.

فأهل كل زمان منهجهم إلى الارتباط بالمصطفى.. خلفاء زمانهم، كذلك رتَّب الله.

أوصاف المرتبط:

قال سيدي رَضِيَ اللَّهُ عَنْهُ: تجد المرتبط.. أمره منضبط، القليل منه.. يفوق الكثير من غيره، اليسير منه.. يتبارك ويحصل به الأثر.

and not in need, he will believe the devilish whisperings that he is not in need, and he will believe all the praises people laud upon him. These are the common obstacles and they all boil down to one thing: he sees himself. When he turns away from the trajectory of the sheikh, the courage of the sheikh, and the path of the sheikh, it will be a means of him being cut off. The Beloved of Allah ﷺ told those who call others to righteousness, 'Convey from me'. In other words, without a break in the connection or chain of transmission. May Allah strengthen our connections and bonds and may He ﷻ strengthen those whom He loves to do that which He loves, the way He loves and may He ﷻ make us among those whom He loves!"

Benefit is proportionate to the strength of connection

My teacher said, "There is no doubt that any person in the *ummah* of the Prophet ﷺ will only benefit from him ﷺ to the extent of his connection to him. Without this, you cannot and will not achieve benefit. There is no benefit without this. All these displays of exertion in spiritual exercises... they are outwards displays. If you find that they have some connection or link to the Prophet ﷺ they will have a positive effect. However, if there is no connection and link to the Prophet ﷺ, they will have no effect. For now, we are in search of people with real hearts and we encourage you to become one of them. We want as many of them as possible and the rest of the required means will come after that, willingly or unwillingly. However, we want the highest stages in the Hereafter".

A murīd should always be concerned about his sheikh

My teacher said, "The right of the sheikh (purely because he is the one who helps you reach Allah ﷻ) who is your door to the chain that links you to Muhammad ﷺ is that you should be like someone sitting on the seashore, waiting for some sustenance to come their way—every time there is the slightest hint of deriving some spiritual benefit from

أوصاف ضعيف الصلة:

قال سيدي رَضِيَ اللهُ عَنْهُ: ضعيف الصلة.. مثل الذي يباهي ويفتخر بالصور بلا حقائق، تَخيَّل الاستقلال أو الاستغناء وتصديق الوسواس.. بأنه غير محتاج، وتصديق الناس في مدحهم له.

هذه عامةُ القواطع وهي راجعة إلى رؤية النفس -أي يرى نفسه — فإذا انقطع عن وجهة الشيخ وهمّة الشيخ ومسلك الشيخ.. كان ذلك سبب القطيعة عنه.

الحبيب صلَّى الله عليه وصحبه وسلَّم قال للمبلِّغين: «**بلغوا عني**» أي بلا انقطاع، الله يقوي روابطنا وإياكم ومن يحب لما يحب على ما يحب حتى يجعلنا فيمن يحب.

النفع على حسب الارتباط:

قال سيدي رَضِيَ اللهُ عَنْهُ: من غير أي شك أن أي فرد من أيامه صلَّى الله عليه وصحبه وسلَّم.. نفعه على حسب ارتباطه، وغير هذا ما حصل ولن يحصل، وغير هذا لا يوجد، وباقي هذه صور الاجتهادات.. صور تقام، إن وجدت فيها الروابط.. أثَّرت، وإن لم توجد.. لم تؤثِّر.

الآن الحث والبحث عن أرباب القلوب نريدهم يتوفرون وبقية الأسباب آتية على رغم أنفها، ولكن نريد عمارة الدرجات العلى.

مراقبة المريد لحال الشيخ:

قال سيدي رَضِيَ اللهُ عَنْهُ: حق هذا الاتصال من الشيخ الذي هو باب السند إلى سيدنا محمد المستند صلوات ربي وسلامه عليه، قال: فيكون كقاعد على ساحل بحر

the special states and moments of the sheikh, either through his movements, his stillness, his appearance, his condition, or his words. The more dedicated he is to waiting for an opportunity to benefit or increase from these different dimensions of the sheikh, the more these moments, glances, movements, and words of the sheikh will be like goblets from which he will drink benefit, and upon which noble spiritual states are based, and by means of which he will be protected from the conniving scheming and plotting of the accursed devil and his own carnal self.

This constant state of waiting will drive him to listen ever-so-carefully to anything the sheikh says. This is a clear indication that speech is one of the keys – when it gets into the hands of the one who understands, the doors of wisdom, recognition, understanding, intuition, spiritual illumination, spiritual states, states of divine ecstasy, unveiling, elevation, and expansion will be opened for him through those words. In this way, the words will become seeds in the fertile soil of the heart and when this seed is irrigated with good manners, etiquettes, and contemplation... they will bear fruit. Some of these seeds will grow into magnificent trees that keep on yielding fruit time and time again, month after month, year after year—the verbal seed that the sheikh had planted in his heart ten or twenty years ago (or more or less) will just keep on yielding fruit. His dedication will lead him to listen ever-so-carefully, hoping to gain some benefit, ever-ready ready to answer, turning to the sheikh all the time, presenting himself for service. Whatever words he is blessed with from the sheikh will prove that he is true in his intention, his quest, and his desire for more grace from Allah ﷻ".

My teacher – may Allah be pleased with him – said, "He should not get too carried away by the gatherings in which poetry is sung in the presence of the sheikh and he should not try to read into it any more than what is obvious from the words that are sung. Unless, of course, he is overpowered by it and the matter is out of his control without any pretence or volition from his side because, in that case, he is excused.

However, as long as there is an element of control and restraint, he should not allow the sung poetry that he hears or anything else to drive him to dancing or moving his body. But why? Some may ask... Abu 'Abdillāh al-Suhrawardi ؓ said, 'Because, by staring at his sheikh, by

ينتظر رزقاً يساق إليه، فكلما تنبه للاستفادة والاستزادة من لمحات الشيخ ومن حركاته ومن سكونه ومن هيئته ومن أحواله ومن مقاله، فكلما تطلع إلى الاستفادة والاستزادة من ذلك.. كانت له ملامح الشيخ ونظراته وحركاته وكلماته كؤوساً يشربها في المعاني، تبتني عليها شريفات المباني، ويُحفظ بواسطتها من شر القاطع الخائن الكاذب الشاني، ومن شر الشيطان ومن شر نفسه.

فتطلعه إلى الاستماع وما يرزق من طريق كلام الشيخ -مشيراً إلى أن الكلام مفتاح من المفاتيح - إذا استلمه من فَهِمه.. انفتح به عليه باب حكمة ومعرفة وإدراك وذوق ونورانية وحال ووجد واطلاع وارتفاع واتساع من خلال هذه الكلمات، فتصير أيضاً بَذراً في أرض القلب، فإذا سقيت بحسن الأدب والتأمل.. أثمرت.

ومنها ما تستمر ثمرته وقتاً بعد وقت شهراً بعد شهر وسنة بعد سنة، ولا يزال يستثمر بذرة كلمة غرسها الشيخ في قلبه قبل عشر سنين أو قبل عشرين سنة أو قبل أقل أو أكثر.

فتطلعه إلى الاستماع طالباً الانتفاع مستجيباً منيباً ملبياً، وما يرزق من طريق كلام الشيخ.. يحقق مقام إرادته وطلبه واستزادته من فضل الله.

وقال سيدي أيضاً: ومن ذلك عند السماع لا ينساق وراء المعنى الذي يطرقه من السماع مع وجود الشيخ إلا إن غُلِب في ذلك وصار الأمر خارجاً عن إرادته، لا بتكلف منه ولا باختيار، فهو في هذه الحالة معذور.

أما ما دام يجد معناً من الاختيار والقدرة.. فلا ينساق مع معاني السماع ولا غيره بالطرب والتحرك، قال لماذا؟ قال -أي أبو عبد الله السهروردي-: لأن استغراقه في الشيخ بالنظر إليه ومطالعة موارد فضل الحق سبحانه وتعالى على الشيخ.. أنجع له في

monitoring the way the grace of Allah ﷻ descends upon him... there is far more benefit and he will be far more successful in terms of purifying his inner self, in traversing the spiritual path quicker, and in perceiving the desired pleasure of his Lord. It is also far more beneficial to him than listening attentively to poetry being sung and getting carried away in the meanings no matter how emotionally arousing or stimulating and no matter how beautiful'.

Reaching the level of absorption in the sheikh, staring at him, and monitoring the descent of divine grace upon him to which the sheikh has indicated, is a physical connection of one being with another. It is one of the most honourable and noble relationships. How can a connection and resemblance of only attributes ever compare? How can the achievement of high spiritual states through rigorous spiritual exercise ever compare?! The reason for this is that when this semblance and inner connection is strong and sound, and when we find this attribute – resemblance to the sheikh and being a mirror image of him – spiritual assistance will flow from the sheikh to the murīd.

However, as long as there is no true affinity, resemblance, or good fit between the sheikh and the murīd together—along with that humility and submissiveness which is like a low-lying valley to which flood waters gush and flow and to which water may trickle or rush proportionate to how low it is—the murīd will be deprived of a great deal of Allah's ﷻ grace and favour. Thus, if the murīd perceives a balance between the meanings he gets from the sung poetry and the spiritual ecstasy he experiences at the time his being is before the being of his sheikh... this is a very lofty state and an incredible bounty from Allah. Nevertheless, the sheikh said that the murīd should not move when he hears the sung poetry while in the presence of the sheikh unless he is completely overpowered and he loses touch with what is happening around him because, in this case, he will be excused.

He – in other words, Abu 'Abdillāh al-Suhrawardi ﷺ – also said, 'The respect and reverence that a true murīd has for his sheikh would prevent him from letting himself go and would restrain him when he hears the poetry being sung' just like it would prevent him from sitting on a prayer mat in front of him. It would prevent him from doing may other things

طُهر باطنه، وفي تقريب الطريق له، وفي إدراكه المأمول من رضوان ربه، و أنجع له من الإصغاء إلى السماع والاسترسال مع المعاني مهما رقَّت وراقت، ومهما طابت له.

فإن اتصاله بما أشار إليه من الاستغراق في الشيخ والنظر إليه ومطالعة موارد فضله عليه.. اتصال ذات بذات، وتعلق في أسمى معاني التعلقات، فأين يأتي منه التعلق بالصفات؟! والتطلع إلى المقامات بالمحاولات من الاجتهادات؟! لأنه عند حسن هذه المقابلة والصلة الباطنة ووجود معنى مما أشار إليه من المجانسة والجنسية للشيخ.. يكون سراية الإمداد من أحوال الشيخ إلى المريد وإلى المتلقي.

ولكنها ما لم تجد المناسبة والمجانسة وحسن القابلية وذلك الخضوع والتواضع الذي يمثل انخفاض المكان الذي يجري فيه السيل فينساق إليه ويمتلئ بالسيل الذي يسيل بحسب انخفاضه شيئاً فشيئاً، فإذا لم يكن ذلك.. حُرم كثيرًا من إفاضة الله.

فما يجده من تأمُّلِه هو للمعاني.. ما يساوي ما يجده من إفاضة الحال عند مقابلة الذات للذات، فذلك فيه معنى رفيع من الجود الوسيع، فهكذا قال: لا يتحرك في السماع مع وجود الشيخ، إلا أن يخرج عن حد التمييز، فهو معذور في ذلك.

قال -أي أبو عبد الله السهروردي-: **وهيبة الشيخ عن المريد الصادق.. تمنعه عن الاسترسال في السماع وتُقيِّده**، كما قيدته عن استعمال السجادة.. تقيده عن أنواع أخر كذلك من الالتفاتات إلى الأشياء ولو كانت عَليَّة عند وجود ما هو أعلى وما هو به أولى.

فإن الكمال.. أن تشتغل بما هو أولى لك وأفضل، لا أن تشتغل بكامل وفاضل، ولكن بما هو أكمل وبما هو أفضل، هذا هو الكمال.

too including getting distracted by other things, no matter how wonderful or important they may seem, because he is in the presence of someone loftier and more important.

Perfection, then, is when you occupy yourself with that which is most virtuous and most deserving. It is not when you occupy yourself with that which is good and important, but when you preoccupy yourself with that which is most perfect and most important. This is the ultimate. This is why some of our elders and pious predecessors have addressed some of the murīds and followers saying, 'O so and so! Have you studied under your father or your uncle or sheikh so and so?' The Mureed would reply, 'I have studied such and such book under them' but the sheikh would reply, 'No, no. I want you to study them (i.e. the teacher), not the books. I want you to study the person he is. Read the sheikh because he is a far greater and far more illuminated book to study, and will have a far greater impact on you'. He – in other words, Abu 'Abdillāh al-Suhrawardi ﷺ –said, 'by staring at his sheikh, by monitoring the way the grace of Allah ﷻ descends upon him... is also far more beneficial to him than listening attentively to poetry being sung'".

When the murīd asks a question, the sheikh is inspired with the answer

My teacher – may Allah be pleased with him – said, "If he does not understand any aspect of his sheikh's condition, he should ask. However, a true seeker does to even have to ask a question verbally in the presence of his sheikh. Rather, his sincerity will be enough to inspire the sheikh to make some kind of indication, statement, or offer some kind of wisdom that would be appropriate to the condition of the murīd and which this murīd and listener needs to hear. Many times the sheikh would say a single word or express a single sentiment or tell a single story... but it will encompass so many meanings that each meaning will appropriately and separately apply to the conditions and situations of those present in the gathering. Some of these stories will save them from a situation they are in, guide them out of a dilemma, open up understanding of the kind of transactions or interactions he is engaging in, or explain something that

ولذا أشار بعض شيبانا ورجالنا إلى بعض المتلقين والمريدين يقول له: يا فلان هل قرأت على والدك هذا أو عمك أو شيخك الفلاني؟

فيقول: قرأت كذا كذا كتب، فيقول له: لا، أريدك تقرأه هو، لم أقصد قراءة الكتب، أريدك تقرأه بنفسه، اقرأ الشيخ، فهذا كتاب أكبر وكتاب أنور، وفيه الأثر الأعظم، وهكذا.

قال -أي أبو عبد الله السهروردي-: **استغراقه في الشيخ بالنظر إليه ومطالعة موارد فضل الحق عليه.. أنجع له من الإصغاء إلى السماع.**

سؤال المريد للشيخ، وكون الشيخ مستنطق نطقه بالحق:

قال سيدي رضي الله عنه:

وينبغي أن يكون تطلعه إلى مبهم من حاله يستكشف عنه بالسؤال من الشيخ، ولكن الصادق لا يحتاج إلى السؤال باللسان في حضرة الشيخ، بل بحسب صدقه يكون مورد إشارة الشيخ وقوله وإفادته متناسباً مع ما يحتاج إليه هذا المريد وهذا السامع.

وربما نطق -أي الشيخ- بالكلمة الواحدة أو حكى المعنى الواحد أو القصة الواحدة.. فانطوت على معانٍ مختلفة تناسب أحوال المتلقين عنه كل واحد منهم على حدة، فيها ما ينقذه ويرشده أو يكشف له عن وضعه وحاله في معاملته أو يُبيِّن له مبهماً عليه في أمر السير، على حسب صدقهم في التلقي، وحسن تنبههم لما له الشيخ يلقي.

وذلك لأن الشيخ يكون مستنطَقاً نطقه بالحق «في ينطق» يقول الله تبارك وتعالى، فيصير الحال إفاضة الرحمن على طالبي التدان، مرسلة من حضرة الامتنان بواسطة أكرم

he had been confused about regarding traversing the spiritual path. All of this occurs proportionate to their sincerity and how well they concentrate and focus on what the sheikh is saying. This is because the sheikh is inspired by Allah ﷻ to say what He 'says', as is proven by what Allah ﷻ says in the hadith *qudsi* 'so, it is through Me that he speaks'. Thus, the gathering is one in which Allah ﷻ showers His grace upon those who seek proximity to Him by sending His special favour via the most honoured of His creation (Muhammad ﷺ) to the tongue of the sheikh currently in their midst. Thus, it is actually as though Allah ﷻ is addressing those who seek to be near to Him and who seek His pleasure via the sheikh. He ﷻ makes these means available so that He can prepare those who truly seek Him for spiritual progress and for ultimately relaxing on the plush carpets of Paradise".

The sheikh is entrusted with the inspiration of the murīd and he follows the Messenger ﷺ in this

My teacher – may Allah be pleased with him – said, "the sheikh is like the custodian of the inspiration that is meant for the murīds just like Jibrīl was the custodian of divine revelation and just like our beloved Messenger, Muhammad, the Chosen One ﷺ from whom this is inherited, is the actual inviter, the one who actually does the spiritual purification, the one who actually explains the intricacies of the path... and the rest of the Prophets and those inferior to them are all just representatives standing in his ﷺ stead, drawing divine assistance from him. The true explainer and clarifier is the Messenger of Allah ﷺ. Allah ﷻ says: '... *for you to explain to the people what has been revealed to them*'. Do you know who 'the people' are? It refers to every single person because each and every person has received some level of clarity regarding the meaning of what has been revealed, so who is the one clarifying it for them? It is the Messenger ﷺ who does not speak of his own desire. In a similar fashion, the sheikh follows the Messenger ﷺ outwardly and inwardly and he does not speak out of his own desire. Speaking of one's own desire refers to two things:

1. The desire to draw people's hearts and attention towards yourself. This does not behove the sheikhs. Rather, it is the trait of defiled,

إنسان إلى لسان الشيخ الحاضر في الآن، وإذا بالحقيقة خطاب من الرحمن يخاطب به طالب قربه وطالب رضاه جاء بهذه الوسائط؛ لُيهيِّئ المتلقي للترقي والجلوس على البسائط.

الشيخ أمين إلهام المريد، واقتداء الشيخ برسول الله ﷺ:

قال سيدي رضى الله عنه:

الشيخ للمريدين أمين الإلهام، كما أن جبريل أمين الوحي، وكما لا يخون سيدنا جبريل في الوحي.. ما يخون الشيخ في الإلهام، وكما أن سيدنا المصطفى صلَّى الله عليه وسلَّم الموروث الذي هو الداعي على الحقيقة والمزكي على الحقيقة والمبيِّن على الحقيقة والمرشد على الحقيقة ومن عدى من أهل التبيين من النبيين فمن دونهم.. نوّاب عنه ومستمدون منه، فالمبيِّن رسول الله ﴿لِتُبَيِّنَ لِلنَّاسِ مَا نُزِّلَ إِلَيْهِمْ﴾ [النحل: ٤٤] تعرف للناس؟! ﴿لِتُبَيِّنَ لِلنَّاسِ مَا نُزِّلَ إِلَيْهِمْ﴾ كل واحد من الناس استبان شيئاً من معنى التنزيل فمن هذا المبيِّن؟! ﴿لِتُبَيِّنَ لِلنَّاسِ مَا نُزِّلَ إِلَيْهِمْ﴾.

لا ينطق عن الهوى، فالشيخ مقتدٍ برسول الله ظاهراً وباطناً لا يتكلم بهوى النفس، وهوى النفس بالقول بشيئين: طلب استجلاب القلوب وصرف الوجوه إليه، وما هذا من شأن الشيوخ ولكنه من شأن الملطخين الموسخين الذين يحبون التفات الأنظار إليهم واستجلاب القلوب إليهم؛ لتعظيمهم أو للثناء عليهم، هذا شأن الملطخين الموسخين، ما هو شأن الشيوخ.

والثاني:

ظهور النفس باستحلاء الكلام والعجب بذلك، وهذا خيانة عند المحققين.

dirty people who like people to see them, who like people to like the so that they can garner respect and praise from them. Only people who have not been spiritually purified and who are defiled (by their base desires) are like this. The sheikhs are not like this.

2. When you enjoy delivering lectures and you like your own voice. According to the scholars, this is deception and betrayal".

When the murīd looks at the sheikh

Sometimes, the hearts of some murīds are filled with such honour and awe for the sheikh that they just cannot bring themselves to completely look at the sheikh. This very condition overcame some of the Companions of the Prophet ﷺ who, out of respect and awe, were unable to look directly at the Prophet ﷺ and see him completely. In fact, one of the senior Companions said, 'I sat with him, I travelled with him, I ate and drank with him, and I spent time in his company for such and such number of years—but if someone had to ask me to describe how he looks, I would not be able to because I could never look at him directly'. This is why the scholars of the Prophetic Biography (*Sīrah*) said that all the narrations that meticulously describe the features of the Prophet ﷺ have been conveyed to us by only two types of people – Bedouins and small children. They are the ones who would carefully stare at the Prophet ﷺ and who then subsequently narrated what they saw to us. As for the general populous of the companions, they could not bring themselves to stare at the Messenger ﷺ out of respect and honour, and this is why they did not describe him to us".

The types of conditions that prevail between the murīd and the sheikh

"The Sheikh – in other words, Abu 'Abdillāh al-Suhrawardi ﵀ – says, 'I used to get a fever regularly. When my uncle, Abu al-Najīb al-Suhrawardi ﵀ would come visit me, my entire body would break out in a sweat and I used to love sweating because it would break my fever. However, this only happened when my uncle would visit me. His visit would be a means of

نظر المريد إلى الشيخ:

قال سيدي رَضِيَ اللَّهُ عَنْهُ:

وقد ينازل باطن بعض المريدين من الحرمة والوقار من الشيخ.. ما لا يستطيع المريد أن يشبع النظر إلى الشيخ.

وهذا الذي نازل جماعة من الصحابة لا يجدون النظر إليه تعظيماً له، حتى يقول قائلهم من سادتنا الصحابة: جالسته وسافرتُ معه وآكلته وشاربته ولزمته كذا كذا سنة، ولو طَلَب مني الواصف أن أصفه.. ما استطعت؛ لأني ما كنت أُثبِّت نظري فيه.

ولهذا حتى قال أهل السيرة: إن الدقة في الأوصاف الخلقية لرسول الله صلَّى الله عليه وسلَّم إنما وردت إلينا من قبل اثنين، مِن قِبَل أعرابٍ أو أطفال، هم الذين كانوا يدققون نظرهم والذين نقلوا إلينا، أما عامة الصحابة فللإجلال والإكبار.. ما كانوا يدققون في هذا أدباً وتعظيماً، ولهذا ما كانوا يصفونه.

أحوال تحصل بين المريد والشيخ:

ويقول الشيخ -أي أبو عبد الله السهروردي- أنه كان يُحَمُّ أو تنازله الحمى، فيدخل عليَّ عمي الشيخ أبو النجيب السهروردي، فيرشح جلدي عرقاً، وكنت أحب العرق من أجل تخف الحمى، لكن أجد هذا عند دخول الشيخ عليَّ، فيكون في قدومه بركة وشفاء، فيعرق من هيبته للشيخ فيذهب عنه الحمى.

وهكذا في ذكر الأدب حتى ما بين الأقران بل ما بين التلامذة والمشائخ، والمشائخ والتلامذة، إذ مرض سيدنا أحمد ابن حنبل فجاء الإمام الشافعي يعوده، فشفى الله

cure and blessings for me'. He would sweat out of awe for his sheikh and, in that way, his fever would break.

There are many such instances of etiquette and manners, even between peers. In fact, even between students with their teachers and teachers with their students! When Imam Aḥmad bin Ḥanbal got ill and Imam al-Shāfi'ī visited him, Allah ﷻ cured Imam Aḥmad bin Ḥanbal. Similarly, when Imam al-Shāfi'ī was ill, Imam Ahmad bin Hanbal visited him and Allah ﷻ cured him. This is when Imam al-Shāfi'ī said his famous couplet:

My beloved fell ill so I visited him
Then I fell ill because I felt so sorry for him
He then came just to visit me
And I was cured just by seeing him!

If this was the respect and honour that a teacher (Imam al-Shāfi'ī) had for his student (Imam Aḥmad), can you imagine the kind of etiquette and respect he showed his teachers?! Here is a prime example of Imam al-Shāfi'ī and his student, Imam Aḥmad bin Ḥanbal. They had a relationship of etiquette and decorum, they had compassion and feeling for one another, and they were sensitive to what others go through.

Abu 'Abdillāh al-Suhrawardi said, 'One day, I was in my home and I had a scarf that my sheikh had given me. He used to tie it around his head. Quite by accident, I stepped on the scarf... I was terribly upset that I had done so, and I was terrified of the possible consequences of stepping on my sheikh's scarf!' The Sheikh added, 'I witnessed such spiritual blessings from the sudden eruption of honour for my sheikh that I could have never imagined'. This incident was a means of him developing a level of respect and awe for his sheikh that he did not previously have. A similar incident is related about the noble Companions who once went somewhere with the Prophet ﷺ. One of them said, 'I would try my best to avoid stepping on his shadow'. Think about it... he would even avoid stepping on a place that was covered by the shadow of the Messenger.

However, when some of the Companions started witnessing more and more of the spiritual light (*nūr*) of the Prophet ﷺ and they found that his

الإمام أحمد بن حنبل ومرض الشافعي فجاء الإمام أحمد يعوده فشفاه الله، فقال سيدنا الإمام الشافعي بيتيه المشهورين:

مرض الحبيب فعدته فمرضتُ من أسفي عليه
فأتى الحبيب يعودني فبرئتُ من نظري إليه

هكذا الآداب حتى مع التلميذ فكيف مع الشيخ؟!

هذا الإمام الشافعي مع تلميذه الإمام أحمد بن حنبل رضي الله عنهما، هؤلاء حاملين الآداب وحاملين العواطف الكريمة والمشاعر العالية الراقية.

فيقول -أي أبو عبد الله السهروردي-:

إني كنت ذات يوم في البيت ومعي منديل أعطانيها الشيخ، وكان الشيخ يجعله على رأسه، فمن غير قصد وقع قدمي على المنديل فتألم باطني من ذلك وهالني وَطْئي بالقدم على منديل الشيخ، قال: وانبعث من باطني الاحترام للشيخ ما أرجو بركته، كانت سبب لأن ينبعث فيه معنى من الإكبار والاحترام لم يكن قبل ذلك.

وهكذا كان بعض الصحابة يمشي مع النبي صلَّى الله عليه وسلَّم، قال:

فجعلت أتحرز أن يطأ قدمي ظله، يخاف أن يطأ برجله على مكان فيه ظل النبي، فلما زاد مشهد بعض الصحابة لنوره عليه الصلاة والسلام صار يشاهد من النور ما يغطي نور الشمس قال: فجعلت لا أجد له ظلاً، أمشي أنا وإياه في الشمس ما أجد الظلال حقه، ظلالي موجود، وظل الأشياء موجود، لكن ظل الرسول لا يوجد، فهكذا كان بعض الصحابة، بينما يشهد البعض ظله فيحترز عن وطء القدم لمكان الظل.

رأيت أدب الصحابة؟!

nūr outshone the light of the sun, one of them said, 'It got to a point where I could not even see his shadow anymore. Him and I would walk outside in broad daylight, but he had no shadow. My shadow, however, was still there and so were the shadows of everything else. However, the shadow of the Messenger of Allah ﷺ was nowhere to be seen'. This happened to some of the Companions while others would see his shadow and try to avoid stepping on it. Can you see the decorum and respect of the companions?! Or are they also going overboard (like some would say)?! Are they also big Sufis?! Do you know more than them?! Are you more intelligent than them?! O Allah! Be pleased with them and inspire us to follow them in the best way possible!"

The way the sheikh interacts with some of the murīds

My teacher – may Allah be pleased with him – said, "When a *murīd* would come to visit Sheikh 'Abd al-Qadir [al-Jilani] and he was informed of this *murīd*, he would open his door only a little, shake hands with the murīd and convey salaam to him, but he would not sit with him. Rather, he would immediately return to his seclusion. However, if someone who was not a *murīd* came to visit him, he would leave his seclusion and sit with him. One of the *murīdīn* disliked that he would not come out to meet his murīds but would come out to meet those he did not know. So the sheikh told him, 'Our connection with the murīd is a connection of hearts, and he is family with no kind of strangeness or unfamiliarity. Thus, our relationship of hearts should be enough for him not to need a physical meeting. The spirituality will make its way to his heart, the *nūr* will reach him and he will rise in rank with this simple meeting in which we shake hands with him. As for the stranger, he is deprived of this kind of connection and benefit. As long as he remains on his old habits and outward practice he will feel affronted if I do not show him some consideration and if I do not sit with him'. Thus, it is the duty of the *murīd* to adorn his outer and inner self with the correct decorum and etiquette in his interactions with the sheikh".

أو هم هؤلاء مبالغين؟! أو هم صوفية كبار؟!

أو أنت أعرف منهم؟!

أو أنت أحسن عقلاً منهم؟!

اللهم ارض عنهم وارزقنا حسن متابعتهم.

تعامل الشيخ مع بعض المريدين:

قال سيدي رضي الله عنه:

أن الشيخ عبد القادر رحمة الله عليه إذا جاء إليه فقير زائر فيُخبَر بالفقير.. فيَخرج يفتح جانب الباب ويصافح الفقير ويسلّم عليه ولا يجلس معه ويرجع إلى خلوته، وإذا جاء أحد ممن ليس من زمرة الفقراء.. يخرج إليه ويجلس معه.

فخطر لبعض الفقراء نوع إنكار؛ لتركه الخروج إلى الفقير وخروجه لغير الفقير، فقال له الشيخ:

الفقير رابطتنا معه رابطة قلبية، وهو أهلٌ ليس عنده أجنبية، يكتفي معه بموافقة القلب ويقنع بها من ملاقاة الظاهر بهذا القدر، وينقدح في قلبه السر، ويصل إليه النور، ويرتقي في الدرجة في هذه اللحظة التي نصافحه فيها،

وأما الثاني فمسكين ما عنده مثل هذا، ما زال مع العادات والظواهر، يستوحش باطنه من عدم الأخذ بخاطره ومن عدم الجلوس معه.

فحق المريد.. عمارة الظاهر والباطن بالأدب مع الشيخ.

The power of a murīd receiving spiritual help from his sheikh

My teacher said, "One of the murīds undertook a journey to meet Habib 'Ali Al-Habshi ﷺ. They travelled a very long way, from city to city, until they finally arrived in Seiyun and proceeded to his mosque, Masjid Al-Riyāḍ. He asked, 'Where is Habib 'Ali?' The people said, 'He will come out for prayer shortly' but the visitor could not wait and he went and stood by the Habib's door. Habib 'Ali exited his home and the visitor conveyed salaam and looked at him. He then bade him farewell, walked away, and set out on his return journey. The people said, 'What a strange man! He has been travelling to meet you for so long, travelling from place to place and when he finally arrived, he only stood for a short while looking at you and then left without even sitting with you?!' The respected Habib replied, 'In those few moments, he got what he wanted and far more. He achieved what he wanted to with the visit because he was sincere in his intentions (for coming here)'".

The murīd should inform the sheikh of that which blocks or prevents him from making progress in his spiritual journey

My teacher said, "We are discussing matters related to both spiritual nurturing and treading the path of spiritual enlightenment, specifically the topic of being deprived of spiritual light. The more you discuss your condition with the sheikh, the more possible it is for you to achieve these two things (nurturing and treading the path) because the sheikh will assist with his spiritual nurturing and he will help him along the path of light. The same would apply to a situation in which the murīd is cut off from others besides Allah and from spiritual darkness (in other words, a very good condition). The more a sheikh is aware of the murīd's spiritual condition, the better it is for his reformation and the more successful the murīd will be in freeing himself from the darkness of his carnal self and all the trials that accompany it. However, if the murīd does not inform the sheikh, sometimes Allah ﷻ will inform the sheikh of some of it. However, the benefit and effect when Allah ﷻ informs the sheikh

قوة استمداد المريد من الشيخ:

قال سيدي رَضِيَ اللهُ عَنْهُ:

وقد سافر بعضهم للقاء الحبيب علي الحبشي وقطع المسافات وتنقل من بلد إلى بلد بمراحل طويلة حتى وصل إلى سيؤون، فجاء إلى مسجده مسجد الرياض، فسأل: أين الحبيب علي؟

قالوا:

بعد قليل يخرج إلى الصلاة، فلم يصبر وذهب ووقف على الباب، فخرج الحبيب علي، فسلَّم عليه ونظر إليه وودعه ومشى وسافر.

قال بعضهم: عجيب الرجل، له في طلبك مدة يمشي من مكان إلى مكان، حتى وقف لحظة ورآك وسافر ولم يجلس، قال: في هذه اللحظة حصَّل مطالبه كلها وزيادة، وبلغ مراده من الزيارة؛ لصدقه في الوجهة.

إخبار المريد للشيخ مما يحجبه في سيره:

قال سيدي رَضِيَ اللهُ عَنْهُ:

فيما يتعلق أيضاً بالتربية والسير سواء بما يتعلق بحجب الأنوار، كلما ذكر ذلك عند الشيخ.. كان أمكن؛ لإمداده بالتربية في مساره في الأنوار، وكل ما كان من حجب الأغيار وحجب الظلمات.. كذلك، كلما اطلع عليه الشيخ من أحوال المريد.. كان أصلح له وأنجح في أن يتخلص من ظلماته وآفاته تلك.

وما لم يذكر.. فقد يُطلع الله الشيخ على شيء منه، ولكن ليس النجاعة والتأثير فيما

and when the murīd explains it to the sheikh himself are certainly not the same. Sometimes, Allah ﷻ conceals and hides the murīd and the sheikh knows nothing about his condition or does not give him any special attention. [Then] there are many other [undesired] spiritual conditions that occur to the murīd, because of which he is deprived of a great deal of progress, and he loses out immensely.

Therefore, when it comes to describing his condition to the sheikh, he should not hide a single negative element or even a single spiritual gift he receives or any supernatural feats or divine responses he experiences. This is to ensure that the murīd is protected from such occurrences that are not truly divine in nature, so that the fake experiences are sifted from the true ones and so that the deficiencies that accompany such occurrences are deflected from him. This will perfect the divine illumination of the occurrences and, by means of this, he will be able to ascend to a higher level among many other benefits.

Abu 'Abdillāh al-Suhrawardi ﵀ also said, 'The murīd should tell the sheikh everything Allah ﷻ knows of his condition. In other words, he should not skip out anything nor should he emphasise the better parts of the information. Rather, he should mention the situation as is, the way Allah ﷻ knows it to be... he should explain it clearly and unambiguously to the sheikh. Whatever he feels too embarrassed about, he should explain in hints and insinuations in such a way that the sheikh understands what he is trying to say. This will be a means of Allah ﷻ taking over and treating him by means of the sheikh and the men in his chain of transmission, or the chain of transmission to Muhammad ﷺ'. He said, 'Because, whenever he does not disclose information to the sheikh, whether it is good or bad, either clearly or by insinuation, he creates a barrier for himself in his spiritual path. Now, he will either be covered in darkness and will not be able to get past the obstacle, or he will be covered in divine light due to which he will not progress within it.

What is required of him is to *pierce the thick veils by sparing no effort in traveling beyond them and to pierce the subtle veils by travelling within them.*

Sometimes the veil and obstacle will be of light, but the murīd halts in his journey when he gets to it instead of traveling within it. Thus, he derives no benefit from that veil. This veil has only appeared for him to

تعرَّض هو لذكره كما جاء من طريق إطلاعه الحق عليه.. واحد، وقد يستره ويكتمه الحق ﷻ ولا يدري به الشيخ أو لا يلتفت إليه، إلى غير ذلك من الأحوال التي تعرِض فيفوت على ذلك السائر شيء كثير.

فلهذا كان في ذكره لحاله.. لا يكتم شيئاً من حاله ومواهب الحق عنده، وما يظهر له من كرامة وإجابة؛ لتُنفى عنه دواخلها، ليُنفى عنه زغلها، ليُنفى عنه ما يعلق بها من النقائص، ليكمل له نورانيتها، ليَعبُر بها إلى ما فوقها إلى غير ذلك من المنافع.

قال -أي أبو عبد الله السهروردي-: ويَكشف المريد للشيخ من حاله ما يعلم الله تعالى منه؛ يعني ما يقصر ولا يتأرجح في ذكر الحال، ولكن تماماً كما يعلم الله منه.. يذكره واضحاً صريحاً للشيخ، وما كان يستحي من كشفه.. يذكره بالإيماء والتعريض؛

ليدخل في حيِّز علم الشيخ وإرادته؛ ليكون ذلك سبباً لتولِّي الله له في ذلك الحال والأمر بمنزلة ذلك الشيخ ورجال سنده أو سنده إلى المصطفى صلَّى الله عليه وسلَّم.

قال:

فإنه متى انطوى على شيء لا يكشفه للشيخ سواء من الظلمة أو من النور تصريحاً ولا تعريضاً.. يصير على باطنه منه عُقدَة في الطريق، فإما أن يُحجب بالظلمة.. فلا يسير عنها، أو بالنور.. فلا يسير فيه.

ومطلوب منه: **أن يقطع الحجب الكثيفة.. بالسير عنها غير مقتصر، وأن يقطع الحجب اللطيفة.. بالسير فيها.**

فقد يكون حجابه من النور فيقف عنده.. فلا يسير فيه، فلا يستفيد منه ولا ينتفع به، فإنما جاء إلا من أجل يسير فيه وبه إلى ما وراءه، وقد يكون من الظلمة فتحِلُّ

either travel within it or to travel with it to another station beyond it. However, sometimes the veil can be a veil of darkness which envelopes him and he does not know how to free himself of it.

It then becomes an obstacle for him in the path to spiritual reformation. However, if he discusses it with the sheikh, the obstacle will be removed and the journey both away from it and within it will be made easy for him'".

The murīd should stick to a single sheikh for nurturing his reformation

My teacher – may Allah be pleased with him – said, "Similarly, the murīd should not enter into the companionship of a sheikh (if the sheikh is able, a good person, and himself reformed) unless he is convinced that this sheikh is able enough and more able than anyone else to reform the murīd. When the murīd has an inclination to this one and that one while in the company of his sheikh, he will not be true in his companionship, the sheikh's words will not have an indelible effect on him, and he will not follow the instruction of the sheikh the way he ought to. In this case, his inner self will not be ready and willing for the condition of the sheikh to settle within him. When he is in the company of the other sheikh towards whom he inclines, he will also concentrate and pay attention to some extent, but it will not be enough for the condition of the second sheikh to settle within him either. Thus, neither will the condition of the first sheikh nor will the condition of the second sheikh make its way into the murīd and, as a result, he will be stuck. On the contrary, if his heart settles on a single sheikh, he will have this opportunity. When the condition of the sheikh overcomes him and settles within him, he is at liberty to take benefit from all the sheikhs out there because he will remain firm on his condition and the channel will be open between him and the sheikh from whom he received this condition or whose condition overcame and settled within him.

Abu 'Abdillāh al-Suhrawardi ﵀ said, 'The more convinced a murīd is that his sheikh is the only one for him, the more he will acknowledge his sheikh's virtue and the more he will love him. When this happens, it will

عليه.. فما يعرف التخلص منها.

فيقول:

يصير منه عقدة في الطريق على باطنه، لكن بالقول مع الشيخ.. تنحَلُّ العقدة وتزول، ويتيسر له السير عن هذا والسير في هذا.

إلزام المريد شيخاً واحداً في تأديبه وتهذيبه:

قال سيدي رضي الله عنه: كذلك لا يدخل في صحبة الشيخ إن كان من أهل التمكين ومن أهل الخير ومن أهل التأديب إلا حتى يوقن ويعلم أنه قيِّم بتأديبه وتهذيبه، وأنه أقوم به من غيره.

فإنه مهما كان في باطنه تطلع في شأن التربية إلى ذا وذاك.. لا تصفوا صحبته ولا ينفذ القول فيه ولا يأخذ الأمر بقوة كما ينبغي، فحينئذ لا يستعد باطنه لسراية حال الشيخ فيه.

ويكون مع الشيخ الثاني أيضاً عنده شيء من التوجه ولكن ما يكفيه فليس له الاستعداد لسراية حال، فلا من حال ذا يسري ولا من حال ذا يسري، فيصير محصور.

ولكن إذا اجتمع قلبه على واحد منهم.. انفتح له المجال، فإذا سرت إليه سراية حال هذا الشيخ، فحسن استمداده من جميع الشيوخ يبقى على رسوخ وعلى تهيئة وعلى قناة مفتوحة له من قِبل ذاك الشيخ الذي فاض حاله إليه، أو وصلت سراية حال إليه وسره عليه.

قال -أي أبو عبد الله السهروردي-: فإن المريد كلما أيقن تفرد الشيخ بالمشيخة..

be because of the love and affinity which is the bridge between the murīd and the sheikh and... in fact, proportionate to the strength of this love, the condition of the sheikh makes it way to the murīd. This is because love is a sign of a familiarity and a familiarity is a sign of a relationship. It is this relationship that will draw the condition of the sheikh in to the murīd. As long as there is no affinity between him and the condition of the sheikh in terms of his readiness and determination, he will draw nothing from the sheikh. He will be deprived of it even if he spends a very long time in his company. The relationship is what draws the condition of the sheikh into the murīd'".

May Allah ﷻ convey His choicest peace and blessings upon our master, Muhammad ﷺ as well as all his Companions, and all praise is due to Allah, the Lord of the Worlds.

14 Rabī' al-Awwal 1434 AH

عرف فضله وقويت محبته، فإذا تم ذلك فلقوة المحبة والتآلف هو الواسطة بين المريد والشيخ، بل على قدر قوة المحبة.. تكون سراية الحال؛ لأن المحبة علامة التعارف، والتعارف علامة الجنسية، والجنسية جالبة للمريد حال الشيخ، وما لم يكن تجانس بينه في استعداده ووجهته وبين حال الشيخ لا تسري إليه السراية، يكون مقطوعاً عنه وإن صحبه مدة، والجنسية جالبة للمريد حال الشيخ.

وصلّى الله على سيدنا محمد وعلى آله وصحبه وسلّم

والحمد لله رب العالمين

تاريخ ١٣/ ربيع الأول/ ١٤٣٤ هـ

Made in the USA
Middletown, DE
10 September 2024

60098930R00061